thinkoneteam

An inspiring fable and practical guide for managers, employees & jelly bean lovers

graham winter

JOSSEY-BASS
A Wiley Imprint
www.josseybass.com

First published 2008 by Jossey-Bass
A Wiley imprint
www.josseybass.com

John Wiley & Sons Australia, Ltd
42 McDougall Street, Milton, Qld 4064

Office also in Melbourne

Reprinted 2008, 2010

Typeset in Palatino LT 11/14.5pt

© Graham Winter 2008

The moral rights of the author have been asserted

National Library of Australia Cataloguing-in-Publication entry:

Author:	Winter, Graham.
Title:	Think one team / Graham Winter.
ISBN:	9780731407880 (pbk.)
Subjects:	Teams in the workplace. Work environment. Organisational behaviour.
Dewey Number:	658.4022

All rights reserved. Except as permitted under the *Australian Copyright Act 1968* (for example, a fair dealing for the purposes of study, research, criticism or review), no part of this book may be reproduced, stored in a retrieval system, communicated or transmitted in any form or by any means without prior written permission. All inquiries should be made to the publisher at the address above.

Printed in China by Printplus Limited

All people, companies and events in this fable are fictitious.

10 9 8 7 6 5 4 3

Limit of liability/Disclaimer of warranty: While the publisher and author have used their best efforts in preparing this book, they make no representations or warranties with respect to the accuracy or completeness of the contents of this book and specifically disclaim any implied warranties of merchantability or fitness for a particular purpose. No warranty may be created or extended by sales representatives or written sales materials. The advice and strategies contained herein may not be suitable for your situation. You should consult with a professional where appropriate. Neither the publisher nor author shall be liable for any loss of profit or any other commercial damages, including but not limited to special, incidental, consequential, or other damages.

contents

To Carol, Mark and Ben

about the author

Graham Winter is a psychologist and business consultant who has worked with top national and international leaders and teams in business and elite sport.

His appointments and experiences include:

- six years as exclusive designer and developer of high performance leadership programs for PricewaterhouseCoopers Consulting in the Asia-Pacific
- three-time chief psychologist for the Australian Olympic Team
- Director of Graham Winter Consulting
- author of *High Performance Leadership* (John Wiley & Sons, 2002)

- designer of the think one team™ and high performance leadership programs.

Over the years Graham has worked with hundreds of organisations, all battling at some point to get past the individual agendas of people and business units to capture the potential of being one team.

Graham consults directly to corporations and through alliance partners who are certified to facilitate think one team™ and high performance leadership programs.

He lives with his wife, Carol, and sons, Mark and Ben, in Adelaide, South Australia.

Graham can be contacted through <www.thinkoneteam.com>.

acknowledgements

Special thanks to my friends and colleagues who helped to bring *think one team* to life as a book and as a successful program for so many businesses:

- Kathy O'Donnell for the countless hours spent refining the manuscript and ensuring that everything about the project is successful. She even gave her name to a jelly bean company!
- Jo West from West Creative for her fantastic design work on all our resource materials
- Mark Winter for being a great sounding-board, a skilled facilitator and a wonderful son
- Nick Wallwork for seeing the potential in this book

- Carol Winter and Ben Winter for believing in me and my ideas
- Frank Prez for professional advice and assistance over many years
- Graeme Alder for his counsel and occasional golf game
- Ron Steiner for his customary feedback, support and sense of humour
- Peter Koshnitsky for his left-field ideas
- Catalyst and Karmabunny for their creativity in designing a great website
- the team at John Wiley & Sons Australia for all their energy and commitment to making *think one team* a great success
- all my clients, alliance partners and colleagues for their enthusiasm and willingness to make think one team a way of doing business.

introduction

Imagine the possibilities when everyone in your organisation thinks and acts as one big team.

This proposition is based on the experience that most organisations (both big and small) are populated by little kingdoms that don't collaborate with each other. Call them what you like—'silos', 'stovepipes' or 'fiefdoms'—they are enemy number one of the business world because they add to costs, irritate customers, frustrate employees, derail mergers and alliances, and are the root cause of countless lost opportunities.

Ironically, it is not the silos themselves that are the problem but rather the inability of organisations, or more particularly the people in them, to foster teamwork across boundaries.

In an increasingly networked world, there is much to be said for giving business units the sort of focus that comes from being a silo; however, few, if any, can genuinely succeed without the ability to open the doors and windows of their silo to collaborate with others on problems and opportunities.

This book and the related think one team™ program have been specifically designed to help you, and everyone in your organisation, to create and sustain the teamwork across boundaries that will enable you to experience the rewards of working as one team.

Beginning with the fable of the big jelly bean team you will join one company's engaging, enlightening and at times funny journey from silo-afflicted to one team. From its experiences you will learn the five practices that define the difference between 'think silos' and 'think one team', and see what these practices mean for leaders and employees across an organisation.

From the vivid story a think one team™ model is built, which you will find easy to understand and apply to your organisation. This model will give you a language to share across the business, and lots of ideas for thinking and acting as one team.

It is important to stress that 'think one team' means being accountable, having clear boundaries and allowing for specialisation. It is not a call to make your business one big department because that will create the poison of bureaucracy. Rather, it is a simple yet powerful message to build the effective and enduring partnerships needed among the people of your organisation to successfully implement the business strategy.

Think one team is a both a mantra and a philosophy of work because it offers a more productive and enjoyable way to live and work.

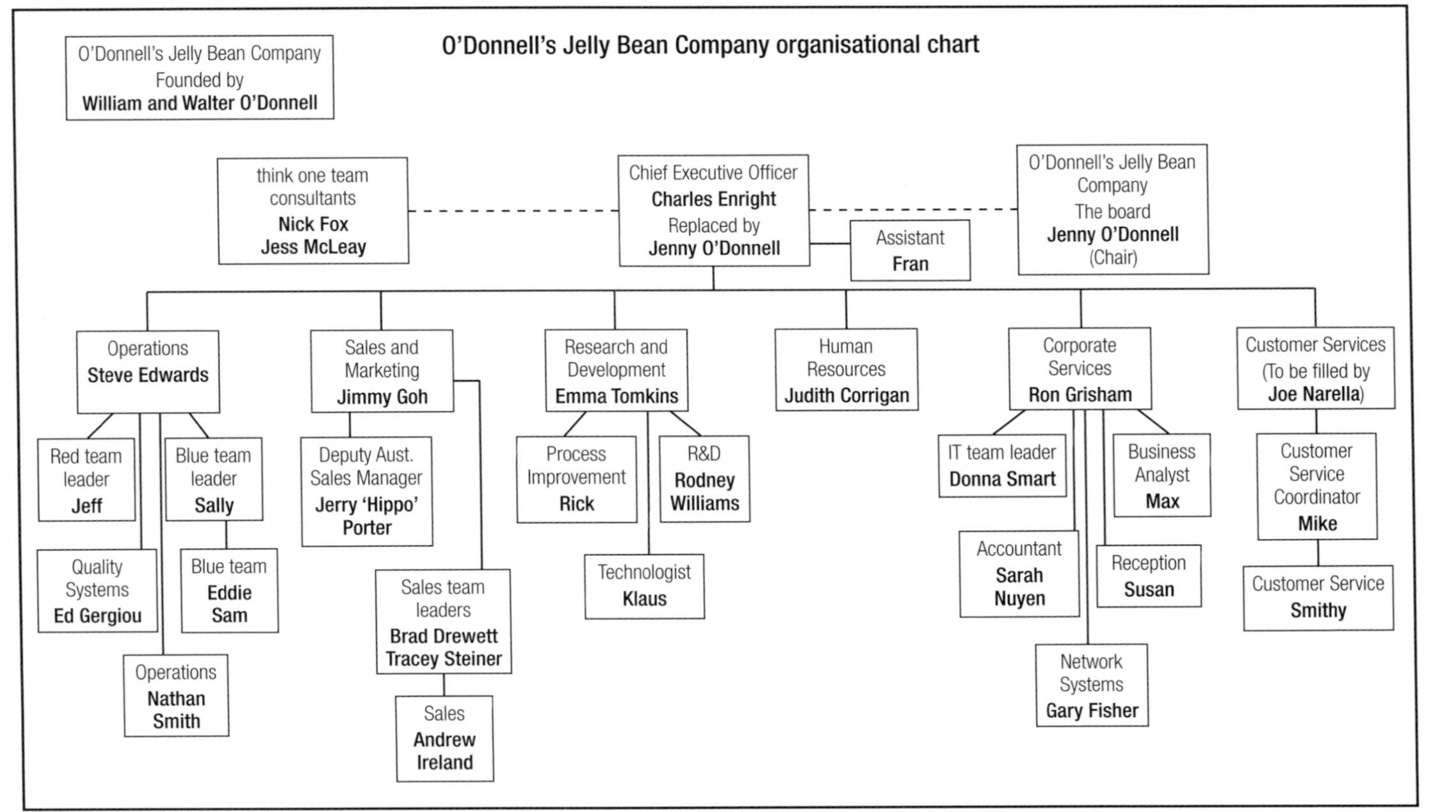
O'Donnell's Jelly Bean Company organisational chart
O'Donnell's Jelly Bean Company Founded by William and Walter O'Donnell
think one team consultants Nick Fox Jess McLeay
Chief Executive Officer Charles Enright Replaced by Jenny O'Donnell
Assistant Fran
O'Donnell's Jelly Bean Company The board Jenny O'Donnell (Chair)
Operations Steve Edwards
Red team leader Jeff
Quality Systems Ed Gergiou
Blue team leader Sally
Blue team Eddie Sam
Operations Nathan Smith
Sales and Marketing Jimmy Goh
Deputy Aust. Sales Manager Jerry 'Hippo' Porter
Sales team leaders Brad Drewett Tracey Steiner
Sales Andrew Ireland
Research and Development Emma Tomkins
Process Improvement Rick
R&D Rodney Williams
Technologist Klaus
Human Resources Judith Corrigan
Corporate Services Ron Grisham
IT team leader Donna Smart
Business Analyst Max
Accountant Sarah Nuyen
Reception Susan
Network Systems Gary Fisher
Customer Services (To be filled by Joe Narella)
Customer Service Coordinator Mike
Customer Service Smithy

the story of the big jelly bean team

Once upon a time, in a now-fashionable inner-city district of Sydney, Australia, a business called O'Donnell's Jelly Bean Company became the market leader in the confectionery industry.

Founded by brothers William and Walter O'Donnell on their return from the Second World War, O'Donnell's Jelly Bean Company was enormously proud of its fifty-year-plus history, its role as an employer of people from the local community and its profitability. Most of all, however, the people of O'Donnell's Jelly Bean Company were proud of its products.

It had been that way since William and Walter produced the first jelly beans in the kitchen of their home in Birchmore Street and sold them to children in the neighbouring streets. 'O'Donnell's', as the business came to be affectionately known, produced the best-looking, best-tasting and best-value jelly beans that money could buy. Any kid who lived near Birchmore Street could tell you that money spent on those monster-sized O'Donnell's jelly beans was a far superior investment to the bland fare at the local store, which carried all the 'brand' lollies. Importantly, an O'Donnell's jelly bean commanded a greater price when on-sold at school. Many children doubled their pocket money by investing in a few of those precious jelly beans and then selling them for a handsome profit at recess. The fame and profitability of William and Walter's jelly beans spread through the schools across the city and in a few months a small manufacturing plant was created at a site that has since grown to accommodate the nearly 500 employees of O'Donnell's Jelly Bean Company.

When you bought 'the real McCoy jelly bean', as Walter loved to call it, you could choose between the three colours (red, blue and black) that O'Donnell's now manufactures in a gleaming, state-of-the-art factory. The enormous jelly beans (about the size of a bird's egg) were sold in clear cellophane packs of five, ten or fifteen containing the one colour of the customer's choice. The first jelly bean ever sold by William and Walter was red, so the teams on the red production line were suitably proud that not only did they produce the lowest cost jelly bean but also that theirs was the original 'real McCoy jelly bean'. The blue jelly bean has always been the most attractive with its sky-blue coating and light-blue inside giving what the blue production teams called 'the sapphire look'. Last but never least was the black jelly bean, which if you asked the black production teams was the most popular choice of customers, the source of much media coverage and clearly a 'better bean'.

O'Donnell's never sold a pack of jelly beans with the three colours combined.

Why? There were three simple reasons and they had stood the test of time.

First, to sell them separately enticed customers to buy more than one pack, and the sales figures supported this view. Many a shopkeeper would tell the story of a mother and her children engaged in passionate debate over the need to buy 'a packet of each' so that the full range of O'Donnell's taste sensations could be enjoyed.

Second, William and Walter always believed that the unique flavours of the three beans would be lost if you put them together in a sealed packet.

Finally, no-one needed to put those jelly beans together because year on year the company grew in revenue, profits and employees.

Until, as they have a habit of doing, things changed.

g'day

They say that Sydney has the most beautiful harbour in the world and it sure looks like it from the left-side window seat as you fly into Kingsford Smith International Airport from the west. The Opera House and 'Coat Hanger' bridge are closer than I'd remembered, and more boats are now sprinkled across the sparkling bays and inlets.

As a forty-something surfer I always think 'sharks' when I see that harbour. Did you know that more people have been attacked by sharks in Sydney Harbour than any other place in Australia? With over four million people living under our flight path I guess that's a lot of potential swimmers and shark bait.

Five years on the road is a long time. Last year I flew the equivalent of twenty times around the planet. Mostly New York to London return, spiced up with the occasional whirlwind trip to Shanghai and Dubai. Leading a consulting outfit is fun but high-demand on everyone and everything.

My speciality is big teams. Not those little departmental teams but whole organisations and big joint ventures—corporations, governments, sporting clubs and associations, universities and even symphony orchestras. If they really want to unleash the phenomenal power that comes from being one big team, then my team will help them to create the teamwork across boundaries that will make it happen.

Australia is home. Not Sydney, actually. I'm originally from Adelaide, a rather English city of parks, hills and stunning beaches. Best place in the world to live. I'll be spending time there getting our next generation of products together ready to take on the greatest of challenges—engaging corporate China to think one team.

I'm Nick Fox. I love jelly beans, Indian food, beaches and the awesome power of big teams.

This story is my way of sharing a few insights from the road about what might just happen to you and your organisation when everyone from the boss to the newest employee lives and breathes the mantra 'think one team'.

chapter 1

real conversations

Tuesday, 8.58 am. The executive team of O'Donnell's Jelly Bean Company assembled for what promised to be anything but the usual 9 am executive meeting.

Walking to the boardroom from their plush offices, the team members crossed a foyer dominated (tastefully) by two identical displays of three two-metre-tall crystal cylinders on either side of the automatic glass entry doors. Each cylinder was full to the brim with those monster O'Donnell's jelly beans—red closest to the street, then black, then blue.

As you enter the O'Donnell's building those jelly bean cylinders escort you like a guard of honour towards Susan, the ever-smiling receptionist. An inconspicuous glass lid sits firmly atop each cylinder to ensure that no-one samples from the display. Floor lights project upwards to complete the striking effect.

By 9 am everyone was seated. Cups of coffee and bottles of water sat on coasters to protect the lush wood-grained table, the compulsory three dishes of jelly beans in the middle of the expansive table and papers at the ready.

Like most businesses, the O'Donnell's executive team was made up of the heads of each of the six key divisions:

- Operations (covering manufacturing and logistics)
- Sales and Marketing
- Research and Development
- Human Resources
- Corporate Services (finance, information systems and administration)
- Customer Services (currently without a head of the division).

The other member of the team, Charles Enright, was appointed Chief Executive Officer less than three years ago through the Sydney old boys' network after an unspectacular reign as head of a brand retailer. The position had become available due to the sudden death of the previous CEO, and Charles's employer had been delighted to give an all-too-glowing reference to a local headhunter who then convinced the O'Donnell's board to offer him the job.

An accountant by profession and with no experience in the confectionery industry, Charles was rumoured to have confirmed more than once to his Saturday golf colleagues that 'O'Donnell's is lucky to have me'. No-one needed the rumour to confirm Charles's arrogance.

Since Charles's arrival O'Donnell's executive meetings had been tediously predictable, with each manager reporting on successes in his or her areas of responsibility and some general discussion about low-level issues such as car spaces and office layout. Anything remotely controversial or strategic (if it was discussed at all) was left to one-on-one meetings behind closed doors with Charles or, if necessary, between the individual members. 'If it ain't broke don't fix it' was a Charles mantra that no-one dared publicly challenge, although, ironically, most people thought of Charles as the most broken thing in the company.

That all began to change early last year when the multinational Jellicoe Candy Corp parachuted into O'Donnell's most important markets, dropping sales by over 25 per cent in just six months. Now, twelve months later, the sales graphs were still heading south and only the cost savings from the first round of bitter redundancies temporarily halted the slide in profitability.

Everyone waited for Charles to open what was expected to be an unpleasant and depressing couple of hours.

He began in a sharp, aggressive tone, with eyes fixed on the table ahead of him, addressing the room rather than his team members in person.

'Yesterday's board meeting was the most difficult in all of my time at O'Donnell's. The board is clearly of the view that the attempts to resolve the downslide of the past year have not been successful and unless this quarter's budget is achieved we will have to cut 25 per cent of costs across the company. I'm personally insulted by the situation and expect this executive team to find answers or heads will roll.'

No-one spoke. For Steve Edwards, head of Operations and the newest (and most articulate) member of the team, it wasn't what he had expected on joining O'Donnell's six months ago, but the business challenge didn't particularly faze him. This was a good business, with good people and good products that were just hitting a few speed bumps.

What concerned him much more than the numbers was Charles's leadership style and its impact right through the business. Steve had seen executives 'burn the furniture' to make the figures look good. Invariably they killed the culture and the company in the process. Charles was a furniture burner if ever he'd seen one.

Steve would bide his time. There were things that could be done, and after three years in a bigger and more complex job in London he more than anyone else in the room actually looked forward to the challenge.

Never one to miss a chance to push his agenda, Ron Grisham, head of Corporate Services and self-appointed 'finance guru', took the opportunity while others were deep in thought to run through the numbers to support Charles.

'Our sales are down over 30 per cent and despite some productivity improvements in Operations I can't see an upside. My view is that we cut now and not wait until the April board meeting.'

Ron looked to Charles for a nod of approval. It wasn't there.

Jimmy Goh, the energetic head of Sales and Marketing, gazed at Ron with a mixture of contempt and anger. This wasn't the moment to tackle Ron's relentless pessimism but he was angry enough to take him on anyway. Just in time, Charles's clipped manner broke his thoughts.

'Jimmy, what's your view?'

A Singaporean national with a Harvard MBA, Jimmy's energy and track record of success with confectionery companies in the United States and Asia earned him respect from all but Ron. As he replied to Charles's question, more than one member of the team was pondering whether Jimmy might soon jump ship for another company with better prospects.

'We've revamped the advertising and PR campaign to be ready for launch early next month, and the customer loyalty program is being upgraded, so I anticipate about a 20 per cent revenue increase on the back of that in the US, Australia and Asia.'

He paused for a moment to gather his thoughts.

'The sales teams are up to the challenge, and if we can improve the teamwork between Sales and Operations, and IT delivers on the customer loyalty platform, I'm confident that we'll claw back what we've lost in market share, and be ahead again within twelve months. I think we need to be careful not to overreact, particularly as the financial information we're getting is way out of date and I think we're already trending upwards.'

'With due respect, Jimmy,' began Ron, running his hands through his thinning grey hair and bristling at the suggestion that his financial information was out of date, 'you haven't got within a mile of any of your sales forecasts for over a year, so why should we believe this one?'

Jimmy leaned forward and looked him squarely in the eyes. 'If you understood the market instead of looking out the back window and telling us where we've already been, you'd know that forecasting over the past twelve months has been impossible because we've had a unique set of circumstances. What do you want me to do? Demotivate the sales teams by setting the bar at a level that you and your super-slow bean counters think we can achieve?'

Ron was no match intellectually for Jimmy and certainly not in a verbal sparring match. He knew enough not to take on Jimmy in this situation. He'd deal one-on-one with Charles and get those cuts in the sales and marketing budget that were long overdue.

Watching all of this unfold was Emma Tomkins, head of Research and Development, and the quietest member of the executive team. She joined O'Donnell's as a food technologist fresh from university and was appointed to her current role two years ago. Emma had been a superb number two in R&D, and very strong in project management and scientific rigour. A clever and insightful scientist, no-one was surprised when Emma, at the age of thirty-two, was appointed to the executive position, although to this day she preferred delving into an experiment rather than leading her small team of highly qualified chemists and technologists. Emma sketched three-dimensional diagrams on the pad in front of her, hoping that someone else would break the silence.

'Charles, are you saying that the board has given us a quarter to turn this around?' enquired Judith Corrigan, Human Resources Executive. She wasn't going to let the meeting deteriorate into a slanging match and, like Steve, she'd seen plenty of worse situations than this during her twenty years in HR and consulting.

'Well, yes', he answered cautiously. 'The Chair and I expect a detailed strategy presented at the next board meeting to address the financial situation. She has also asked me to meet her separately this morning to go over our three-month interim strategy.'

Despite Charles's reputation of dismissing anyone who overstepped their authority or disagreed with him in public, Judith was determined to press forward with her point of view. 'Okay, we seem to have two options: either we do as Ron suggests and start working on more reductions now or we back Jimmy to lift the sales performance.' Not waiting for a reply, she turned to Steve. 'You've led a company that hit a hurdle and then picked itself up again. What do you suggest?'

Steve was taken aback that Judith had tossed the ball to him. He'd only been in the job a few months and apart from the newness he was acutely aware that Charles seemed threatened by his experience, which had been in a similar job to the one that Charles had failed in prior to joining O'Donnell's.

All eyes focused on him, wondering whether he'd been tossed a ball or a hand grenade. It was a moment for leadership and Steve was both a natural and a well-developed leader.

He turned respectfully to Charles. 'Can I have a few minutes to work us through some ideas that I think are important?'

Charles couldn't refuse without looking weak. 'Just a few minutes, we have a lot to cover', was his muted attempt at keeping the upstart Steve Edwards under control.

real conversations

If you really want to know how a business is travelling don't go to the boardroom, go to the staff canteen.

People in boardrooms can lose connection with what actually makes the organisation tick. They miss the conversations, the emotional moments and the open tensions. Things are often controlled in boardrooms because of status and agendas. Steve knows that, but he's courageous and skilful enough to take the risk and bring a dose of harsh reality to Charles, Ron and his colleagues that they'll never get from a set of accountant's figures.

But first to the canteen and to the conversations that tell us what is really happening in O'Donnells.

the staff canteen

Meanwhile in the canteen staff milled around the coffee machines, while two eager players pounded a table tennis ball at each other in the far corner of the long rectangular room.

Production had started at 6.30 am so Jeff, Sally (team leaders in the red and blue production teams, respectively) and Mike (the Customer Service Coordinator) were more than ready for a strong cup of coffee and a biscuit. They had joined O'Donnell's on the same day five years ago and had kept in touch through a shared interest in tennis, which they played most Tuesday evenings in summer for the social club.

Mike and Jeff strolled halfway to the table tennis players and sat at one of the thirty or so round laminated tables.

'How're things?' asked Sally, pulling up a chair and reaching for the sugar pourer.

Jeff put down his coffee mug.'Pretty crap, actually. We're way down on production volume and everyone's scared that more redundancies are around the corner.'

'Yeah, same with us, although I hear that Sales is forecasting a big jump next month', Sally offered optimistically.

'That would be the same forecast they got wrong last month', added Mike sarcastically. The others nodded unenthusiastically in agreement, although both knew that Mike was a sniper who enjoyed spreading gossip, particularly if it was bad news. And they weren't about to be proven wrong by his next comment.

'I hear it's going to be a council of war at the exec meeting today. Davo from finance reckons that Ronnie Grisham's going to nail Jimmy about the forecasts and has you guys in his sights for some serious slash and burn.' He paused to smirk before adding, 'At least it would be good if something came out of an exec meeting instead of the secret club just keeping it all to themselves'.

Sally and Jeff could only agree with his last point. While their new boss, Steve Edwards, seemed to be making every attempt to keep them updated on what was happening, there had rarely been anything that showed them where the company was heading. It was just small-picture stuff about their own department and mostly negatives about everyone else. 'Like putting a jigsaw together when there's no picture', Jeff had remarked at a recent meeting.

They sat quietly for a few moments. Sally's thoughts were on the mess-up with materials that she would have to fix when she went back to work. The Purchasing Department had decided that it could get a great price on red colouring, so without consulting with the production teams it had spent the entire monthly budget on red colouring. Now blue can't meet its targets for the week, while red is oversupplied and, as Jeff said, slowing down.

Mike didn't know it yet, but three of O'Donnell's customers, including the biggest specialist confectionery chain, were expecting the blue jelly beans for in-store promotions and would be on his case within twenty-four hours. Fortunately for Mike he knew a way to put the heat back on Sally and the IT Department even though he'd promised yesterday that everything was running to plan.

'Better get going', announced Jeff standing and heading towards the dishwasher, and passing two staff members who were furtively polishing their resumes, which they would forward to local recruiters in the next week.

'See you', Sally and Mike replied together, before making their way back to work.

current reality

Back at the executive meeting Steve stood and strode to the electronic whiteboard that hung on the far wall of the boardroom. Unclipping a black marker pen he drew a straight line down the middle of the board, dividing it into two equal columns. At the top of the left column he wrote 'Old model' and on the right-hand side 'Current reality'.

Turning to face the team, Steve began with an open question: 'What are the key ideas that drive our business?'

Emma's scientific mind immediately wanted to clarify exactly what Steve was after.

'Do you mean, like Nike's core idea is to produce shoes that make people winners and McDonald's is to mass-produce fast food?'

'Exactly', replied Steve with an encouraging smile. 'Successful businesses have a core idea and then lots of related ideas that support it. I'm interested to know what you think ours are.'

'We make jelly beans', offered Ron, not quite understanding where this was heading but wanting to control it if he could. Judith nodded and then added, 'Quite right, and I'd add that we aim to make the best jelly beans in the world'.

Steve jotted a summary of Judith's words in the 'Old model' column and turned again to the team. 'Fine, I think we'd all agree with that idea. So, what are some of the other ideas that tell us how to go about achieving that?'

After twenty minutes of increasingly lively discussion (during which Charles added just one brief comment but Steve certainly had his full attention), and some writing and rubbing out on the whiteboard, a list of five points sat underneath the statement, 'Our core idea is to make the best jelly beans in the world'. Those points were:

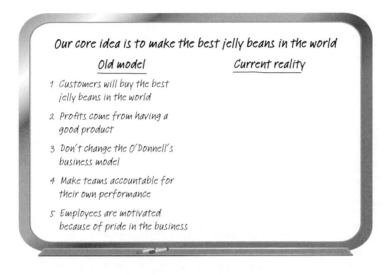

Our core idea is to make the best jelly beans in the world

Old model	Current reality
1 Customers will buy the best jelly beans in the world	
2 Profits come from having a good product	
3 Don't change the O'Donnell's business model	
4 Make teams accountable for their own performance	
5 Employees are motivated because of pride in the business	

Steve scratched his chin and smiled as he looked at the list. 'If William and Walter were here today, I think they'd wholeheartedly agree that these are five compelling reasons why the business has been so successful for over fifty years. Do you agree?'

Everyone nodded, except Jimmy who had been uncharacteristically quiet since his run-in with Ron.

Steve pointed to the 'Old model' list. 'Unfortunately, like most business ideas these were right for the past, but they are all wrong now.'

Charles was furious at Steve's criticisms. With blood pressure rising, his mind was yelling, 'How dare you tell us what is wrong with a successful business that you virtually walked into yesterday!'

He now understood why he'd been so resentful when Jenny O'Donnell, the board Chair and daughter of William, had recommended Steve for the Operations job. 'Steve the upstart' was taking over the meeting and the team. This would stop as soon as Charles got him into his office on his own.

open and honest

O'Donnell's is a great example of a business that doesn't have open, honest and constructive debate at the senior management level.

Instead of tackling the tough issues, they have leaders like Charles who use their status to aggressively stifle debate and others like Emma who avoid conflict at all costs.

Having the courage and skills to tackle the tough, constructive conversations is one of the first and most important steps in creating the united leadership, which is the foundation on which big teams flourish.

Sensing an opportunity to ingratiate himself with Charles, Ron began to object but Steve cut across him determined not to let the moment be lost.'Just a minute, Ron, please let me finish my line of thinking and then we can fully debate it.'

Charles noticeably turned his body away as Steve started writing in the 'Current reality' column. Ron fumed, Emma wished the meeting would finish and Judith wondered just how this leadership team could ever be united enough to pull the company out of the looming crisis.

When Steve had finished, the whiteboard looked like this:

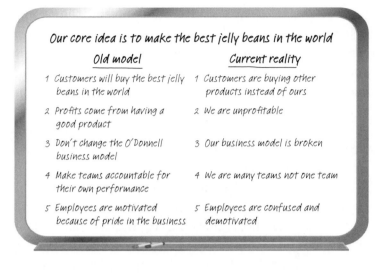

Our core idea is to make the best jelly beans in the world

Old model	Current reality
1 Customers will buy the best jelly beans in the world	1 Customers are buying other products instead of ours
2 Profits come from having a good product	2 We are unprofitable
3 Don't change the O'Donnell business model	3 Our business model is broken
4 Make teams accountable for their own performance	4 We are many teams not one team
5 Employees are motivated because of pride in the business	5 Employees are confused and demotivated

Even Charles tuned in as Steve slid onto the chair at the end of the table and spoke quietly and sincerely to the team.

'I joined this team six months ago because I liked what I'd heard about the culture of O'Donnell's and its potential. In that time I haven't seen anything to suggest that O'Donnell's doesn't have a great future, but we have to create that future, because the world has changed and we can't just let things drift along as they are.

'There is no doubt that the last batch of redundancies and the other cuts were needed, and in my opinion, without those we would have slid even further. But it doesn't address the real reasons this company is in danger of failing completely.'

Charles bristled and glowed a deep red colour as Steve continued in a calm but assertive tone.

'There are two things that this company does not do and they are killing us.

'The first is teamwork. We aren't a team. From this executive team through to every operational team, we compete against each other for budgets, for resources and for recognition. We work in little teams with our own agendas and we protect our own turf at all costs. Just go to a Sales and Operations meeting or a project review and you'll see that we don't really collaborate with each other, we don't constructively challenge each other and we don't work as partners towards shared goals.

'The second is communication. We rarely listen to each other and we certainly don't listen to customers and understand what they really want. We just make our brilliant jelly beans and try to convince everyone that all is fine. But the reality is that people are not buying our jelly beans and we don't seem to be learning from that.

'It seems to me that we have two paths. We can wither away slowly in our departmental teams and silos or we can get rid of the roadblocks to communication and teamwork that we are putting in our own way. If we take the second path, I genuinely believe that we can become a greater company than William and Walter ever conceived, but it will demand united leadership from this executive team and a new culture of teamwork across O'Donnell's.'

Steve had said everything that he wanted to say and a bit more. Silence hung in the room as each executive took in the personal and business implications of his message. They also wondered how and when Charles would react.

Charles's immediate need was to take back control, but he wouldn't risk tackling Steve head on in the meeting. 'Steve, thank you', he muttered bluntly, packing up his papers and bringing the meeting to a premature halt. 'You've given us much to think about and that's what I'd like to do. I have a meeting with Jenny O'Donnell at 11 am so Steve you and I will meet in my office at 1 pm. We'll reconvene this executive meeting at 3 pm.'

Charles expected to have Steve's resignation to announce by that time.

Ron followed Charles out the door, while Judith congratulated Steve on his presentation. Emma and Jimmy left separately, each deep in thought about their own careers.

arrogance hides something

The best leaders have long passed the stage where they need to strut arrogantly around the business. Arrogance is usually a sign of low emotional intelligence or lack of confidence—or both.

Either way, a business is never going to fulfil its potential if that is the way of the people in charge. They'll soon find that everyone just strokes their ego and lets them do all the thinking. That might work in the short term but it's a recipe for disaster in anything but a one-person business.

When the time comes to choose new leaders at all levels, look for humility and self-confidence, backed by a drive to get things done. Steer clear of people who constantly need their tyres pumped up. They're likely to go flat just when you hit the toughest terrain.

jumping ship

Shortly after the meeting ended, Jimmy hesitated, then quietly knocked on the door before entering Charles's office. He had planned this moment for later in the week but events were gaining momentum and he wasn't comfortable keeping the news from Charles while such important issues were being discussed. He respected Charles for his financial skills but found his ego overpowering. Not surprisingly Jimmy was much more concerned about bailing out on his team and colleagues than the self-centred CEO who had rarely commanded loyalty from anyone in his business career.

Standing in front of Charles's desk, and in a subdued but definite tone, Jimmy explained the approach by a headhunter and the job offer that was simply too good to refuse. He hadn't been looking for another job but sometimes things just happen. What Charles didn't know, and Jimmy couldn't tell him, was that two of his top account executives were almost certainly leaving with him.

Charles slumped into the leather chair behind his desk. 'Where are you going?'

Jimmy shook his head. 'Sorry but I've signed a confidentiality agreement, which means that I can't disclose it until I start there in six weeks' time.'

Charles shrugged, not really caring where Jimmy was going. If he'd known that it was Jellicoe Candy there wasn't much he could have done, but he would have demanded that Jimmy leave immediately.

'I'll have to tell the executive team this afternoon', Charles announced sombrely. 'Sure, that's your call', replied Jimmy, feeling the urge to apologise but knowing that it didn't make sense to say you are sorry for something that you really want to do.

a new o'donnell

Jenny O'Donnell served five years on O'Donnell's board before succeeding her Uncle Walter as Chair on his passing twelve months ago. A lawyer and Chief Executive of one of Sydney's better known legal practices, this was her first experience as a chair, although many years specialising in corporation law was an excellent grounding.

There were three rules that Jenny lived her life by:

- Be clear about your intentions.
- Act decisively with courage.
- Give and expect respect.

They were what her father had drummed into her from her earliest years and they hung on her office wall as a daily reminder. These three principles had helped William survive the war and build a successful business. For Jenny, they would guide her to rebuild what William and Walter first created.

Charles had seen the plaque on Jenny O'Donnell's wall but taken no notice of it. Had he reflected on the three rules he might have better understood what she was about to tell him.

Jenny arrived a few minutes early and chatted briefly to Susan at reception before being ushered into Charles's office. Their meetings were always slightly formal affairs. Charles was of the era that didn't take easily to reporting to a woman, and certainly not to one whom he believed inherited the role, not earned it. Jenny, by contrast, gave and expected respect, which never seemed easy with Charles.

'Charles, the board held an extraordinary meeting last evening to discuss the company's situation.' Charles was stunned by the news that the board had met without him. 'We have not taken this decision lightly, but we have made the decision to seek your immediate resignation.'

Jenny waited for a reaction. Charles went bright red and was soon gasping for breath.

Charles would recover from the panic attack, although being carried by ambulance stretcher across the foyer watched by startled employees wasn't what either he or Jenny would have wanted. That was perhaps the only thing on which they agreed, as Jenny sat quietly in the now-vacant chief executive's office and pondered the next steps in her plan to revive O'Donnell's.

chapter 2

values 24/7

O'Donnell's was abuzz with rumours, mostly exaggerated but all tinged with an excitement that maybe, just maybe the company would be rid of the arrogant, pompous Charles Enright.

Sales staff emerged from cubicles eager to hear the latest bulletin on Charles's condition, production teams milled around sharing the juiciest gossip and even the studious finance team huddled together sharing a joke at the Chief Executive's expense.

Certainly not too many people were upset by Charles's horizontal departure through the foyer, and the words 'Total Eclipse!' scrawled across the whiteboard in the sales meeting room captured the mood of many who were of the view that Charles sincerely believed that the sun rose from his own backside.

Depending on where you walked around the company, Charles was variously dead from a heart attack, had been paralysed by a stroke, had choked on a ham sandwich or had even been punched out by Jenny O'Donnell, although the last theory was more wishful thinking than believable.

No-one knew that Charles had been sacked or that an O'Donnell was again about to lead the business. There were plenty of surprises coming and even a few that Jenny O'Donnell wasn't expecting.

a new reign

Jenny O'Donnell sat at the CEO's desk as her father had years before, knowing that the future of the business rested in her hands.

Reaching for the phone, she punched in a local number and waited.

A relaxed Australian accent tinged slightly with an American twang answered almost instantly. 'Morning, Nick Fox speaking.'

'Nick, Jenny O'Donnell here', was the more serious reply.

'Hi, Jenny, nice to hear from you. How's Sydney's brightest and best legal mind this sunny morning?'

'Nick, I'm fine but it's not a legal matter that I'm calling you about.'

When something was particularly serious Jenny had a habit of beginning her sentences with a person's name and Nick knew her well enough from their time working together in New York to spot this and shift to business mode.

He listened intently while Jenny rattled off a quick yet detailed account of O'Donnell's recent history. It was the brief you would expect from a good lawyer: succinct, structured, punctuated with facts to support the main themes and culminating in a summary of the key points and actions.

'The grapevine tells me that you're not back in Australia looking for work, Nick, so I can fully understand if this is just a catch up call and we head off in separate directions.'

She paused, while Nick waited and wondered what Jenny had in mind.

'I really need some help to turn this business around. It's a great business and I'm sure it wouldn't surprise you that the current problems are more to do with culture than numbers. Nick, this is a great team waiting to be unleashed, and that's your bread and butter. Can you spare some time to give us a kick-start?'

Nick's plans for the next six months were more about writing a book and generating some new thoughts and creative energy before launching the think one team venture in China. Getting involved in a jelly bean company in Sydney wasn't exactly in his frame, but something about this appealed.

Besides, Nick liked Jenny and had huge respect for her integrity and business skills. He decided he would help her if he could.

'What if I jump in a cab and we catch up for half an hour to at least tackle the communication to staff issue?'

'That would be great', she replied warmly. 'Can you be here around 1 pm?'

'Sure can. I'll see you then.'

From the beach-side apartment that he had rented for a week to catch a few waves and do some business, it was only a short drive to O'Donnell's. Nick knew the layout from many years ago when he interviewed Jenny's father while doing some of his initial research work on big teams before heading off to the United States.

As he sat in the taxi reflecting on the best way for Jenny to cut through all the rumours and give her staff a clear corporate signal, the new Chief Executive was already notifying the executive team to meet in the boardroom at 3 pm. If things went well, it would be their first introduction to Nick Fox and her intention to turn O'Donnell's from its many and varied silos into one big, formidable team.

His thoughts were soon interrupted as Nick found himself standing between cylinders of blue, red and black jelly beans that ushered him towards the still-smiling Susan.

you are only a new boss once

When I took over one of the first teams in my business career someone advised me that 'you are only a new boss once'. Unfortunately, there is a difference between being told something and actually listening!

Six months into the job I realised that I hadn't had the conversations with my team that clearly defined the 'rules' of the game that we were all playing. The conflicts and misunderstandings showed a serious lack of leadership on my part. I'd missed the chance to shape the important things, to create a clear big picture while still new, and as the newness wore off it seemed ten times more difficult to change.

Jenny has that window of opportunity of between three and six months to set new expectations and standards for O'Donnell's. If she hasn't had an impact by that time, she'll also learn the hard way that you are only a new boss once.

1 pm, coogee beach, sydney

Sam and Eddie sat outside the breaking waves waiting for one last wave to finish what had been a great surf session.

The offshore breeze had stayed soft but steady all morning and there was no hint that a sea breeze would ruffle the still solid one metre swell that was barrelling over the sandbars.

'What do you reckon?' asked Eddie, the evening-shift Maintenance team leader for O'Donnell's blue team.

Sam, a leading hand on the blue team, was much more interested in extra surf time than the evening shift at O'Donnells. 'We could just paddle in and call in sick in the next twenty minutes', he replied.

'You can't just call from the beach — the seagulls will give it away', laughed Eddie, spinning his board and stroking hard as a larger swell started to lift fifty metres seawards. 'See you on the beach.'

They both caught the same wave, with Eddie the more senior at work and on a wave getting the clear water, while Sam got crunched as the wave ledged on the shallow inner sandbar. Shaking the sand from a shaggy mop of jet black hair, Sam jogged, board under his arm, to join his colleague at the small pile of clothes and towels on the dry sand.

'You know, I'd never have done this three years ago', said Eddie to the slightly distracted Sam who was watching a lifeguard, rescue board in tow, dashing towards a swimmer who was flailing helplessly in the rip. 'Yeah,' grunted Sam, 'but it was a good place to work then because everyone got on'.

'That mongrel Enright stuffed it up for everyone', mused Eddie to himself as Sam attempted to towel his unruly hair.

'I say we go up behind the Coogee Hotel, find a quiet spot and each call in to HR', suggested Sam. 'You can have food poisoning and I'll have a migraine.'

'Bloody hell!' exclaimed Eddie, staring at the text message on his mobile phone from one of the day-shift maintenance guys. It read: 'Enright's dead or something. Chaos here. Suggest you stay at beach. See you at Coogee pub at 7.'

Twenty minutes later they'd both called HR to advise of their sudden illnesses and were rewaxing their boards in anticipation of another few hours in the now-rising swell.

'They don't treat us like we're part of a team, so I reckon we deserve a day off occasionally', yelled Sam as he ran at the shore break and skilfully jumped feet-first onto his board and slid up over the crashing wave. Eddie wasn't quite as cynical as Sam, but like a growing number of O'Donnell's staff, sick leave was a way to bring some fun back into what had become a daily grind. And no-one wins when people lose their passion for a company.

He paddled out along the rip line, dodging a couple of surfers flicking off at the end of their rides, and leaving it to others at O'Donnell's to scramble through the evening shift without their usual maintenance cover.

tough love

Over the years, Nick Fox and his team had devised a short, sharp set of core principles to guide managers and team leaders to lead a think one team initiative. One of those principles, 'never leave a vacuum', alerts leaders to be vigilant in preventing any communication gaps between management and key stakeholders, such as staff, business partners and owners. When things are changing, people soon create their own (usually false) rumours if that communication is missing.

Nick had heard himself countless times encouraging leaders to 'never leave a vacuum'. It was a double-edged principle for leaders: 'Send crystal clear messages. Listen first so you understand what things look like from others' perspectives.'

Charles Enright would have choked on his muesli over the expression 'listen first', but Jenny O'Donnell knew what it meant.

Within thirty minutes, Jenny and Nick had crafted a brief note to all staff advising that Charles's health was fine and that there would be an all-staff meeting addressed by Jenny at 4 pm the next day in the canteen (coinciding with shift change).

Most of the staff knew Jenny through the regular plant visits that she had insisted on, despite Charles's irritation at having the board Chair strolling through *his* business. Her pleasant and professional style had seemed such a contrast to the arrogant Chief Executive's superior airs and, of course, some of the longer serving staff knew her as a child, so there was a natural affection for her and a connection to a time when O'Donnell's was like one big family.

This was now a family that needed some 'tough love' but one thing could be assured—there would be no leadership vacuum while Jenny O'Donnell was in charge.

on the team

'Nick, I'd like you to attend the executive meeting at 3 pm if you have the time.' Jenny paused and waited for his reaction, then continued when he agreed. 'There are so many things that this business has been doing wrong over the past three years and one of the most important is that we've destroyed a lot of the good things about the culture without replacing them with a better option.'

She filled in a few more gaps including how, unbeknown to Charles, a subcommittee of the board had spoken privately with three members of the executive team (Judith from HR, Steve from Operations and Jimmy from Sales and

Marketing) and with the best intentions for the business each had been willing to share their views on the current reality of the business.

Jenny preferred not to go behind the back of the CEO, however, she and other board members had suspected that Charles was putting a positive spin on a deteriorating situation. The discussions had only heightened her concerns, hence her urgent recommendation that was accepted by the board last evening to fire Charles and replace him with Jenny.

3 pm executive meeting — end of the spin

The executive team sat motionless while Jenny briefly introduced Nick as a facilitator with a role that she would explain later.

Nick sat back from the table while Jenny confirmed that Charles's condition was not serious, and then immediately hit them with the bombshell that the ailing CEO had been asked to resign by the board. She stressed that her first step in getting more honesty and openness into the business was to confront reality and not put a spin on it—Charles had led the business poorly and was not up to the job.

Had the team been fitted with heart-rate monitors, it would have been Ron Grisham's that was pounding the fastest as he worried who was next in the board's sights.

Jenny continued, aware that no-one in the room wanted to discuss anything as yet.

'The board has asked me to take the role of CEO, commencing immediately.'

Two executive panic attacks in a day would be unlikely, but Ron was as close as you get when trying to sit impassively at a board table while your career flashed before your eyes. Nick thought Ron's complexion matched the red jelly beans.

'There are three immediate pieces of business to address, so let's cut straight to the issues.

'First, I want everyone to be totally clear about what I see as the big picture for O'Donnell's.

'Second, there are critical short-term business issues with cash flow and customers that must be fixed.

'Third, I want to fully introduce Nick Fox, who will guide us as we reshape the culture of O'Donnell's.

'After that I will meet with each of you individually in my office, starting immediately after this meeting, to agree on what we expect of each other and to discuss your role in taking this business forward.'

leap of faith or burning platform

Jenny was about to lead a major change at O'Donnell's that would upset power bases, abolish entrenched practices and fundamentally alter the day-to-day work of many people.

Despite the challenges faced by the company, people do not easily embrace this level of change unless there is a strong, logical case and an equally strong emotional case to discard the past for a new future. The 'indisputable need for change' as one of my clients calls it.

The logical case is easy. Most leaders can explain logically why their business could or should improve things such as customer service, speed to market, consistency of processes and so on. It's creating the emotional case, the motivation to act and withstanding the challenges that's the key. That motivation might come from fear and loss ('the platform is burning so we'd better jump') or pleasure and gain ('let's leap into a bigger and brighter future').

Most corporate initiatives fail because they don't create an emotional case to challenge and change the status quo. Sometimes that's about inspiring words and actions, and sometimes it's about setting fire to a few platforms.

Over the next thirty minutes Jenny told the story of how William and Walter created O'Donnell's Jelly Bean Company, and of the values that underpinned the business. She spoke of passion, of their first foray into large jelly beans and the creation of a cook, pack and ship production line that revolutionised the industry. She described their fanatical concern for integrity in the product, and of how they instilled a discipline in the manufacturing and selling of the product. Finally, she spoke of teamwork and the pride that William and Walter felt as people approached them seeking to work at O'Donnell's because of the strong team bond, the supportive management and the fun workplace.

Her voice was tinged with a fierce resolve as she told how O'Donnell's had lost its way.

'Instead of integrity and discipline we've created a boring "me too" business that any MBA student could reproduce in a week.

'Instead of teamwork we're making an art form out of competing against ourselves for budgets, time, resources and people.

'And any sense of passion and fun seems to have been squeezed out of the place.'

'Look at the wall', she said, pointing to the values poster that hung next to the whiteboard. Everyone turned to look at a rather jaded-looking poster with the words 'integrity', 'passion' and 'teamwork' on it.

'Our values are on the wall but they don't mean a thing. I've spoken to quite a few staff over recent months and, to put it bluntly, they think the values are a joke.

'So, starting from this moment we return to our roots to build a new future. As the leaders of O'Donnell's, each of us is accountable every moment of the day to drive passion, integrity and teamwork back into the heart of this company.

I expect you and I to live, breathe and be the values twenty-four seven. They will become our trademark as a united leadership team.' She paused for effect then turned towards the visitor. 'And that is why I've asked Nick Fox to join us.'

values 24/7

You've probably got values posters on the wall in your organisation, but do the values genuinely mean something to you and the people you work with on a day-to-day basis?

A set of values, or a 'team code' as it is called in sport, is absolutely essential to creating a flexible, high-performing outfit. It's too slow to rely on rules and regulations—you've got to be able to trust people to use the values to guide their decisions when they're under pressure.

The journey for O'Donnell's, and I'd suggest for your business, is to instil specific and meaningful values that people live their lives by 24/7—not switch on and off when they walk through the door every day.

Jenny was impressive and Nick couldn't help but be caught up in the energy of her ideas and determination as she began his detailed introduction.

'Nick and his team specialise in coaching and guiding organisations to change from acting like lots of small disconnected teams and silos to making teamwork a competitive advantage. Steve, I think you know Nick from some work that he did with you in London?'

Steve nodded. He was a fan of think one team because the simple model and tools engaged everyone and could be built into the business systems instead of being just another fad.

Jenny continued, 'Nick, we've got a great company. But we've lost our belief in what we can become. I know that you and your team have lots of things happening, but we'd really appreciate your help'.

All eyes turned to their guest. Steve caught his eye and shrugged. Nick knew he was hooked.

'Sure,' he replied immediately, 'it sounds like fun'.

divided we fall

A week earlier, Jenny O'Donnell had sat alone in the Qantas lounge at Sydney airport waiting on a delayed flight to Melbourne.

Two O'Donnell's sales team leaders, Brad Drewett and Tracey Steiner, were sitting in nearby lounge chairs and Jenny couldn't help but overhear their conversation. Tracey was upset about something at work, and Brad was agreeing with her.

'Sales seems to get the blame for everything in this place and yet just look at how other people screw up.' Brad nodded as she went on. 'If IT had their act together we could actually be prepared when we get in front of clients instead of them knowing more about O'Donnell's than we do. I mean, how embarrassing was it last week in Singapore when I was told by the client that we were two weeks behind on delivery? You can imagine the chances of hitting budget on that account.'

'Couldn't agree more', added Brad before joining in. 'And what about new products? Do you think there's any chance they could get within ten kilometres of a customer before telling the world about their next wonder product?'

'No more likely than Marketing sharing the promotional campaign with us before we start getting calls from clients about discounts that some genius in head office has promised them', replied Tracey.

There was a tension in her voice that sounded a lot more serious than a gripe session among colleagues. 'Which is why I'm out of here as soon as another job comes along.'

Brad laughed. 'Yeah, that's assuming that HR can process your resignation in time!'

Jenny cringed. She was sure that O'Donnell's wasn't as bad as the conversation suggested, but these were two of the key people on the talent pool list that went to the board last month, so if talent is unhappy enough to walk out the door, then she knew there were big problems.

no spectators

Did you notice how Brad and Tracey have become negative spectators in their own company?

One of the challenges for every organisation is to engage people so they don't end up thinking and acting like negative spectators at a tennis match.

Spectators are dangerous in businesses because they see themselves as above the game and either can't or won't take responsibility for fixing things. They see problems as negatives instead of improvement opportunities, fortify the walls between departments and layers of hierarchy, and suck the energy out of the people who really want to give it a go.

Converting spectators into players is everyone's job because you won't create a one team culture if you can't get people to collaborate to solve problems across the boundaries.

Pause and reflect for a moment: how many people in your team or organisation are more 'spectator' than 'player'? Which are you?

setting the highest bar

Jenny, Nick and the executive team gave themselves less than twenty-four hours to prepare for a presentation to all staff, so every minute was vital.

Nick headed off with Judith to get the quick-fire briefing on the business that he needed before running an introduction to the think one team program for the executive team in the morning. In the back of his mind he was still wondering whether getting involved with O'Donnell's was going to be a distraction from preparing the next generation of materials for China. He'd give it a week because he was in Sydney for that time anyway, and then see how things were progressing.

Not surprisingly, Jenny was fully prepared for the one-on-one meetings with each executive and first-up was Ron Grisham. It was Jenny's choice. As was the agenda.

Forever the 'control freak', Ron immediately offered to go over the finances but Jenny quickly made it clear that she knew enough about that for the moment. 'I don't intend to discuss the numbers, Ron. My interest today is how you and I might work together in the future.'

Charles's narcissism had been a perfect place for a bully like Ron to hide. He enjoyed doing Charles's bidding knowing that threatening to drag a fearful staff member into the Chief Executive's office was the quickest way to get what you wanted. Ron didn't see himself as a bully, but Jenny did and that sort of behaviour didn't fit with passion, integrity or teamwork.

In fifteen business-like minutes, Jenny outlined her expectations, described the behaviour she did and did not expect of her immediate team and clearly, almost surgically, explained to Ron the toxic effect of his behaviour on the culture of the business. Finishing on a more positive note she praised his technical skills as a finance manager and offered to support him to develop his people skills. But there was a caveat—it had to be fast-track improvement or she would replace him. No second chances. Ron left shell-shocked and with much to consider.

One by one each executive received the same clear, unequivocal message: no-one is more important than the three core values—passion, integrity and teamwork. There was no direct threat in what Jenny said. It was a statement of fact that left no doubt that she intended to set the highest bar on everything for herself and the team.

go one-on-one

Leaders lift the attitudes, emotions and behaviours of other people. If you can't do that, then you can't lead.

Few people have the charisma and substance to inspire from the soapbox, but even the quietest of leaders can be incredibly powerful in one-on-one conversation.

As a general rule (whether you are CEO or a first-time team leader), the more time you spend in one-on-one coaching discussions with your team (without micro-managing) the more success you'll have as a leader.

The final one-on-one meeting late in the evening was with Jimmy Goh, the Sales Manager who had resigned almost twelve hours earlier to a person who was carried out on a stretcher and no longer worked in the business. He was gobsmacked with what Jenny said before he even sat down.

'Jimmy, I know that you are leaving us and I am very disappointed.'

'Charles told you before he collapsed?' Jimmy asked in surprise.

'No, your future employer isn't very good at keeping a secret', she replied bluntly.

Jimmy was at a loss for words.

'There are many board members who understand your frustration with Charles and Ron. In fact, your impending departure was one of the final straws that broke the camel's back for the board last night and led to the decision on Charles.'

Even though he'd taken his eye off the ball a bit over recent times, Jenny knew the business desperately needed a person of Jimmy's capabilities, energy and experience. Certainly she didn't want him playing for the opposition, and she set about convincing him to reject the offer from Jellicoe Candy. It was close to midnight when Jimmy agreed to give it more thought and then to have a further discussion after the staff meeting. Jenny hoped that the combination of the session with Nick in the morning and the full staff meeting in the afternoon might build enough momentum to push Jimmy to go back on the offer.

Jimmy was angry that the confidentiality on his new job had been broken by his future employer. Maybe with Jenny in charge it might be a better option to stay; he was too tired to make a career decision at that time of night.

chapter 3 

the one team question

It was a weary executive team who gathered around the boardroom table at 9 am on Wednesday to hear what Nick Fox had to say. Joining them were ten managers and team leaders from across the business who had been personally asked by Jenny to attend and openly participate.

Their attendance was just one of many steps that she would take to unlock the 'executive club' and get teamwork happening across the horizontal and vertical boundaries of O'Donnell's.

'Morning, everyone', Nick began with his customary openness.

There was barely a flicker from the group and he knew that their minds were elsewhere on the unfolding turmoil in the business.

'Have you ever heard of the Three Kingdoms?'

It was a hook, intended to capture their attention and it worked immediately as Jimmy responded, 'It's a part of Chinese history'.

'It is', replied Nick, 'and it's repeating itself in O'Donnell's and in most twenty-first-century organisations'.

Now he had everyone's attention but only for as long as he promised to be part of the solution and not a distraction.

'Let me briefly explain.'

Nick flicked a slide onto the projection screen showing a typical Chinese scene and recounted the story of the period in Chinese history following the Han Dynasty (a period of stability and unification) when the great country was divided into three smaller kingdoms, each of which developed their own laws and ways of life.

A good storyteller, he had everyone's attention as he described how for 300 years from approximately 220 AD, China's three kingdoms fought each other, and even though there were periods in that time when China was unified, this quickly fell apart again. He highlighted that this tension created many good things, such as beautiful art and strong local communities, but it was characterised by countless battles and loss of life (and much romanticising of the heroic generals and their armies). Crucially, the culture that was China was all but lost in this period.

Nick continued, 'Most organisations go through periods like China's Three Kingdoms where, for often quite good reasons, they split into kingdoms that become more important to the members of that kingdom than the overall organisation. People build their departmental fortresses, lose sight of the bigger picture and even create a mythology around the heroes who do battle and win inside the organisation. The business loses its culture and fails to grow to its potential.'

find the right metaphor

People love metaphors because they reduce complex ideas to simple, memorable concepts.

The story of the Three Kingdoms is a great example of this process, and hopefully the big jelly bean team is an even better one!

Through the metaphor of the Three Kingdoms, Jenny and the rest of the O'Donnell's leaders could easily see how and why this style of 'silo thinking' can be so damaging in the way it encourages internal competition, duplication of resources and loss of culture.

Choose your metaphors wisely and use them often to master the art of motivating people to take on challenging tasks in difficult environments.

fast forward

Nick would experience the realities of the O'Donnell's kingdoms in a few days when invited to attend the quarterly budget review meeting. You would hear fewer arguments outside an English football game, and even with Nick as an obvious outside observer, a conversation between two staff from Sales and Operations became so heated that an offer to sort it out in the car park was almost taken up.

Many a legendary story in O'Donnell's had its birth in these regular budget review meetings that pitched one department or function against another and became a battle for survival, and at times an opportunity to bludgeon an unsuspecting manager into giving up some of his or her budget.

A favourite story of many was when Ron Grisham banned all capital expenditure except the architectural redesign of the corporate suite that housed Charles and Ron. Not to be outdone, some very creative unnamed Sales staff took it upon themselves to form a mysterious construction company, which then tendered for the work at such a low price that they won the business. Using unskilled and unemployed people from the local labour exchange, they completely stripped Charles's and Ron's offices, before winding up the company and sending letters advising that the company was insolvent and the proprietors had fled overseas.

The purchasing manager only survived because he was able to find one of the conspirators, but everyone enjoyed the three months that Charles worked in an office without a ceiling or carpet.

hitting the spot

'The Three Kingdoms sounds like our manufacturing plant with the three jelly bean lines', commented Ron. He didn't intend to be malicious but it roused Judith who observed dryly, 'And I think we have some bigger kingdoms when we look at Sales, Operations and Corporate'.

'Can't disagree with that', replied Ron to Jenny's pleasant surprise.

'Are there other kingdoms in O'Donnell's?' enquired Jenny in the hope of flushing out some of the hidden truths.

Donna Smart, a recently promoted team leader in Information Technology, surprised everyone by rattling off one area after another, 'Purchasing, Payroll, Customer Service, Production Planning, Marketing, Quality Systems, Accounts Receivable, New Products, IT, etcetera, etcetera'.

'And then cut it the other way', added Max, a business analyst. 'We've got the board, then the executive, then their direct reports who are sort of a management group, then team leaders, operations staff and contractors. The boundaries are pretty thick between those levels.' Just about everyone nodded.

Nick smiled. 'The Three Kingdoms is a useful metaphor because it helps us to see that organisations are almost genetically programmed to split into kingdoms, and it stays that way until all the leaders—from CEO to team leader—start to think and act differently.'

He paused to make a crucial point. 'It is important to understand that there is nothing wrong with creating separate business units. You need boundaries and clear accountabilities between areas, but when the boundaries block communication so the company can't service customers and quickly respond to change it's time to build teamwork across those boundaries.

'That is the essence of think one team. Not creating one big department but rather building partnerships that create and sustain teamwork across the boundaries.'

be accountable for the value stream

People often want to know whether they should focus on their own business unit or think as one team, but this isn't an 'a' or 'b' answer.

Both are important in a networked world because we need people to be accountable to deliver their projects, their service or their products, and we need them to partner with others in the business along the line that specialists in lean manufacturing (based on the Toyota Production System) call the 'value stream'.

We often launch think one team programs alongside lean initiatives and the thing I like the most about lean are the value-stream maps that start with the customer and work their way back through the business. These maps are a great way to show people how their work links with others to create value for customers and the business. Importantly, the value-stream maps also show what doesn't have to be linked and therefore avoids wasting time and resources on links that don't matter.

and then along came joe

Thousands of kilometres away at London's Heathrow airport, Joe Narella, a second-generation Australian, born of Italian immigrants, was waiting in the Qantas lounge to board his flight to Sydney and his new role as Customer Service Executive for O'Donnell's Jelly Bean Company.

Headhunted by a prestigious executive recruitment firm, he had been interviewed by Charles via videoconference and offered the job that would allow him to return to Sydney and the young family that he had seen all too infrequently since working in London as export manager for Charles's former employer.

It had been a whirlwind few days but he was impressed at how quickly O'Donnell's had made its decision and he looked forward to meeting the rest of the team on his arrival.

They might have thought the same except that Charles had not involved HR in the recruitment process, so no-one apart from the headhunters and Charles's assistant Fran knew that he was on his way. Fran didn't get the nickname 'The Rottweiler' for nothing, so it was highly unlikely that she'd be giving up that little piece of information until it was in her best interests to do so.

Getting blindsided on recruitment was something that Judith had become used to, as few O'Donnell's managers bothered to involve HR in their hiring decisions, preferring instead to wait till the last minute and then demand that all the paperwork be processed immediately. Ironically, even before meeting Nick Fox she had complained to Steve that managers ran their business units 'like their own little kingdoms'.

defeating three kingdoms thinking

Across the top of the whiteboard Nick scrawled the words 'Five practices to defeat Three Kingdoms thinking' and underneath wrote 'Think silos' and 'Think one team'.

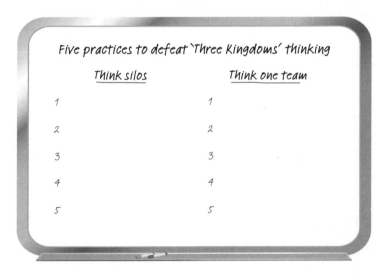

Five practices to defeat 'Three Kingdoms' thinking

Think silos	Think one team
1	1
2	2
3	3
4	4
5	5

'Is everyone familiar with O'Donnell's attempt to launch the green bean last year?'

There were groans, nods and a few laughs all round.

Many years of consulting had taught Nick the art of quickly finding the best in-company example of three kingdoms thinking and it didn't take too many chats with team leaders and operations staff around the canteen and car park to pinpoint 'Project Green Bean' as the perfect culprit.

Just about everything that could go wrong had gone belly-up with the attempt to launch a fourth colour jelly bean the previous year. The green bean was described in the national newspaper (with some accuracy) as 'tasting like cats' urine', however, this gave Charles, who enjoyed any chance to strut his stuff in the media, the chance to deny the claims on the *Sunday* business program. Unfortunately, he met his match in a smart young journalist who enquired how he actually knew what cats' urine tasted like. Charles's answer still appears occasionally in TV bloopers highlights (and was a top-five hit on YouTube), but the green bean was gone before breakfast the next day and sackings followed quickly afterwards.

Nick pointed to the whiteboard. 'There are five fundamental differences between "three kingdoms thinking" and "one team thinking". Let's look at what these five differences mean in practice to see if they show why Project Green Bean may have hit the wall.'

big picture or separate agendas?

Nick wrote on the flip chart that stood in the corner next to the whiteboard:

Pursue other agendas |————————| *Share the big picture*

He explained, 'It's human nature that people are motivated and directed by their most important agendas. In the vast majority of organisations there isn't a big picture or a big agenda that is more important than the individual agendas within the "kingdoms"'.

'You see this in places like universities where every faculty thinks its is the most important, or in the countless corporate head offices where arrogance is matched only by their ignorance of what things are really like in the field. Think about the thousands of useless bureaucratic rules coming out of head offices and the energy that goes into complying with them, or the wasted money on new information technology that doesn't work because no-one asked the people who actually do the job!

'Think about the phone companies, power suppliers and big banks that you deal with. Do the people you contact in those businesses really know the big picture, or are they just one of the individual parts that don't know what the others are doing?

'And how many times have you heard the rhetoric about "whole of government" but rarely see two government agencies working together to solve a complex social issue? They do the opposite and then make heroes out the leaders who get more money out of treasury for their pet projects. It's crazy and it's so like the generals in ancient China who became heroes by destroying each other.

'When people genuinely think one team, they all commit to something that they can't achieve individually but they can achieve collectively. That's a big picture, not the little agendas that we've been discussing.'

Nick gave a few examples of one team thinking and then sat at the table and quietly but firmly turned the spotlight on the group. 'Most of you were a part of Project Green Bean and if not, I'm sure that you've all heard a lot about it, so please take a pen and mark the point between "Pursue other agendas" and "Share the big picture" that you believe characterised that project.'

When they all sat down again every mark was as far away from 'Share the big picture' as possible.

meanwhile ...

Once a year Lollies on Parade!, one of Australia's largest confectionary retailers, decorates each of its twenty Sydney shops for its 'Into the Blue' promotion. Blue streamers and balloons, bright blue flags and even a blue carpet announce to the public that there are prizes to be won, including around-the-world travel, new cars (blue of course), hundreds of blue T-shirts and every imaginable type of blue lollies.

In the middle of every shop window a wheel designed to fit O'Donnell's sapphire-blue jelly beans into numbered slots gives a stunning visual appearance as it spins and lands on a number that sends a lucky customer 'Into the Blue'. Tomorrow morning there would be queues stretching along shopping malls across Sydney. Into the Blue is one of the most popular and high-profile promotions in the harbour city.

Everything was ready for the launch except that over the past hour trucks had started delivering O'Donnell's jelly beans to each of the twenty shops and the phone was ringing hot in the office of Tania O'Dea, head of Marketing for Lollies on Parade! Angry franchisees demanded to know why they had received box upon box of bright red jelly beans to put in their Into the Blue window displays.

A livid Tania gave up trying to contact the O'Donnell's executives, who seemed to be in endless meetings. Being only a short drive away, Tania soon thundered through O'Donnell's reception, past a still-smiling Susan, straight into the boardroom, interrupting Nick's presentation and throwing everyone into confusion.

Four hours later, after turning the place upside down, the first run of sapphire-blue jelly beans made its way along the production line and into the waiting trucks.

'It's amazing what we can do when there's a crisis', commented Sally as her blue team kept check on the line and corrected some minor temperature issues in the extruder. It was all hands on deck with even a few R&D people helping on the line to fast cook the beans and check quality.

Mike drifted past in the background wary not to get caught in the crossfire between Purchasing and Operations. He could have stopped them cancelling the order for blue colouring this week and preventing the inevitable problems with Lollies on Parade! but usually the customer puts up with it and in any case, his performance review is due next week and the savings will ensure that he hits his financial targets. And that, as Charles has said or implied many times, is more important than anything else. 'Maybe I'll even get a bonus for this', he mused to himself as he sauntered off to the car park leaving others to sort out the mess.

The afternoon staff meeting had to be reluctantly postponed by Jenny so that the Lollies on Parade! order could be filled.

the one team question: 'What is best for the business?'

When was the last time you heard someone in an important meeting ask, 'What is best for the business?' This is a one team question and it resonates with growth and success.

Sadly, it's not par for the course in the corporate world for all sorts of reasons. For a start, there's competition for status and resources at every level and in every area. In some organisations if you give up something it can be seen as weak, so everyone holds onto information, money and other resources so they make their kingdom look best.

Often a break point is needed, like a crisis or disaster that forces people to look at the whole picture and not just their little piece of the jigsaw. Ideally it isn't necessary to mess with destruction and instead that's when united leadership can make a difference.

Irrespective of whether you are a team member, team leader, manager or senior executive you have a responsibility to think about the big picture and not to push another agenda. The best way to begin doing that is to regularly ask the fundamental question, 'What is best for the business?'

In O'Donnell's, the way that the senior managers deal with the consequences of Mike's inaction will also be an interesting insight into how serious they are about being on one team.

back in the boardroom

With the blue production line spilling out sapphire jelly beans, Steve and Jimmy were able to convince a still-fuming Tania that she'd have blue jelly beans spinning in all twenty of her Lollies on Parade! window displays by morning.

Reconvening in the boardroom, Nick enquired, 'How does what we've just seen over the past few hours and your experience with Project Green Bean relate to agendas and sharing the big picture?'

'They're both perfect examples', confirmed Jimmy. 'We have people who think they own the customers, so their agenda is control and to keep people out. In Project Green

Bean they kept R&D away from the customers and even though the recipe matched all the specifications, people didn't want to buy green jelly beans because of both the taste and colour. We could have stopped the project and saved millions if only we'd known.'

Emma added, 'R&D has to share some of that responsibility because our agenda is to make the most technically perfect product. So I guess we are sometimes less interested in what the customer thinks than what the science tells us'.

Ron mused to himself that none of the financial analysts really focused on Project Green Bean because their selective loyalties were to the red, blue and black production teams.

'That's an interesting insight,' reflected Nick, 'and typical of the Three Kingdoms where they created three governments all with duplicated roles'.

'We do that', chipped in Rick, a Process Improvement Engineer. 'Each production line has its own accountant, chemist and marketing people, so it's not surprising that new ideas and best practices fall over because they can't bust through the silos.'

Judith added, 'Come to think of it, we actually recruit people to fit our kingdoms instead of the overall business'. It was an 'aha' moment for the HR manager.

'So what should have been the big picture?' Nick asked.

'The same as we've just seen in the last two hours with the Lollies on Parade! crisis', replied Jimmy. 'Everyone working together to give our customers the O'Donnell's experience, which means great products and great service.'

Nick was delighted with the team's energy and insights but knew that he had to keep them firing right through all five practices so he cut short the discussion, wrote the first practice on the whiteboard and moved on to the second practice.

Five practices to defeat 'Three Kingdoms' thinking

Think silos	Think one team
1 Pursue other agendas	1 Share the big picture
2	2
3	3
4	4
5	5

share reality or avoid and deny?

Nick showed a series of quotes from top performers in world-class organisations across the fields of business, sport, emergency medicine and even an Everest expedition.

He paraphrased the common message: 'High-performing individuals, teams and organisations crave feedback'.

'Why?' he asked rhetorically before answering his own question. 'Because without it they can't stay safe and achieve great things.'

He contrasted this with what happens when people think 'kingdoms' and compete against each other.

'You get low trust and it's much harder to get at the truth. You hear sugar-coated conversations in which people avoid the hard truths and put a spin on things. That means lots of blind spots, which put the business at risk.'

On the flip chart, where Nick had written the second set of practices, the group marked their scores and again all were positioned well to the left.

Avoid and deny |————————| *Share the reality*

'Project Green Bean was a classic example of putting a positive spin on everything instead of calling it like it really was', ventured Max, the Business Analyst. 'Every department kept telling us how well its part of the project was progressing while no-one said what they really thought.'

'Which was?' asked Nick.

'It was a great product that no-one wanted to manufacture, sell, buy or eat', replied Tracey, one of the sales team leaders, laughing at how ridiculous this sounded.

Nick knew the answer to his next question but wanted to see if someone was prepared to tell the truth.

'How did it get that far?'

Ron sighed and gave every indication that he was about to speak. Finally, he broke the silence. 'Because it was Charles's idea and no-one had the guts to tell him the truth.'

'Thanks, Ron', replied Nick, 'that's one of the most honest things I've heard anyone say for a long time'.

Ron flickered an embarrassed smile. He wasn't accustomed to being open in meetings or to having someone praise him in public. With a violently alcoholic father he'd learned at a very young age how to make himself invisible by concealing his emotions. It was a survival technique then and had been more than helpful in navigating the tantrums of the equally dangerous Charles.

Jenny was pleasantly surprised to see Ron's openness and wondered if perhaps he did have a future at O'Donnell's after all.

more reality

In the pause that followed Jimmy decided that the meeting could go no further without sharing the reality of his resignation speech to Charles and his discussion with Jenny.

'Is it a done deal?' asked Steve, breaking the uncomfortable silence that followed Jimmy's admission.

'Well, it was yesterday', replied Jimmy. 'But I'm disappointed with the way Jellicoe Candy handled the whole recruitment process and, to be frank, the main reason I was leaving was Charles and now he's gone.' He paused and looked at Ron but decided against commenting on the difficulties that the head of Corporate Services had created for him.

'Does that mean you'll reconsider?' asked Judith, pressing the point.

'Please give me until morning. I'll have a final answer then', replied the rather ill-at-ease head of Sales and Marketing, wanting to chat things over with his wife, Limei, before making a final decision.

'Okay, let's meet after the staff meeting', suggested Jenny, expecting him to stay but still not totally confident that he would.

cyb (cover your backside)

As the discussion resumed, Judith reminded everyone that each Friday an HR staffer emptied the suggestion box that had sat for twenty years in the entrance area to the canteen. Over the past six months the two most popular suggestions were to fix the flood of internal emails and for Charles to do something that he would find physically impossible to do.

While the latter comments were always discreetly shredded, Gary Fisher, the ever-suffering Network Systems Administrator (great title for an awful job), had been working for some time on a strategy to stop the email war that was engulfing O'Donnell's.

Among the suggestions were to add another category after 'cc' and 'bcc' to the emails, so that when people felt the need to copy others on an email they had to decide whether there was a good reason or if it was just to cover their behinds. Judith's suggestion that 'cyb' be added to the system so people might show some courage by admitting their behind covering behaviour brought a much needed laugh to the group.

A few more minutes of sharp discussion and the group had grasped the idea that 'share the reality' was not about blaming but about wanting and actively seeking feedback, being prepared to confront reality and knowing that a certain amount of conflict is healthy.

Nick kept things moving.

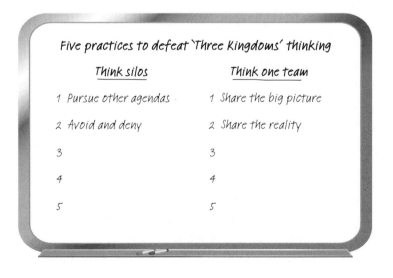

Five practices to defeat 'Three Kingdoms' thinking

Think silos	Think one team
1 Pursue other agendas	1 Share the big picture
2 Avoid and deny	2 Share the reality
3	3
4	4
5	5

share the air or stifle communication?

In a now-famous moment in the history of 'Project Green Bean', the former head of Operations had managed to convene a sixty-minute meeting attended by fifteen people in which only three (including himself) spoke. Someone remarked later that there were more spectators at that meeting than at Saturday's national league football game.

Project Green Bean had all the hallmarks of three kingdoms thinking:

- the person with the loudest voice and most power (or both) dominated meetings
- there were few if any two-way conversations between the key players
- chronic hoarding of information was a feature at every stage.

'We couldn't get a word in at project meetings and in the end there just wasn't any point in attending', commented an exasperated Emma.

'It was the same for us', revealed Donna from IT. 'Everything we suggested hit a brick wall of cynicism so there was no point. To be honest, we just put the project on the bottom of our priority list and nothing got done.'

Jenny was thinking about her own experience in a legal practice in which she had worked earlier in her career. The combination of a rigid hierarchy and personality clashes at most levels had stifled the creativity and energy of new graduates, who either learned to shut up and do what they were told or left to pursue their careers elsewhere.

She recalled that any views that even slightly challenged the status quo were discarded in a way that was probably more habit than intention. The most common phrase at meetings was 'Yes, but' and this deflated Jenny who had been raised to put her viewpoint even if it was challenging to those in authority. She didn't stay long, but it was a good lesson in how not to run a business.

After a few minutes' discussion the marks on the flip chart were again pushing hard to the left and everyone could see that O'Donnell's had lost the openness of communication and sharing of ideas that characterised its earlier years.

Stifle communication |————————| *Share the air*

buy spectators a parachute

'Stifle communication' has two sides to it.

The person who dominates the airwaves is probably the most obvious (and annoying) destroyer of both big and small teams. However, managers and specialists who quietly hoard information aren't far behind in the damage stakes because they take the oxygen out of the room.

The walls of corporate silos are thickened by managers and technical specialists who use knowledge for the power it gives them or who simply won't speak up when it's needed. This happens inside businesses and also in so-called alliances.

When you see that behaviour, call it. These people are the airline passengers who see smoke coming out of the engine and say, 'Hey, it's not my responsibility'.

Buy these spectators a parachute and get them off the plane: they are a danger to everyone, including themselves. Don't put up with the 'oxygen thieves' either.

Nick suggested a short break before completing the final two practices.

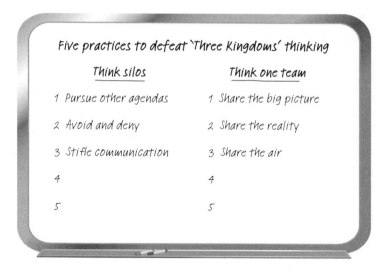

Five practices to defeat 'Three Kingdoms' thinking

Think silos	Think one team
1 Pursue other agendas	1 Share the big picture
2 Avoid and deny	2 Share the reality
3 Stifle communication	3 Share the air
4	4
5	5

share the load or look after your own turf?

Most of the group used the break to visit the blue production team to see how things were progressing. While they were yet to discuss the fourth practice, 'share the load', it confronted them immediately as they walked into the production area.

R&D staff were still there hours after their usual finish time, people from Sales were helping to seal the special blue packages and maintenance staff from black team were filling in for yet another person on a fake sickie. Even two IT staff were arriving with pizzas to feed the troops.

'Is this how it normally works?' asked Nick, slightly tongue in check.

'Not likely', replied Jimmy. 'On a normal day it's nothing short of a union demarcation in this place. You get quite good teamwork inside the departments but no-one shares the load outside their areas. They don't think about it and they don't know what people do anyway.'

Nick recounted a recent experience with a consulting firm where the partners and managers made an art form out of not sharing their load across or down through the firm.

They never planned or prioritised together, they made everything much more complicated than it needed to be and no-one ever thought to look left or right from their job to see what was happening along the line.

Clients wore the negative impact of the firm's silos and took out their frustration on the less senior consultants doing the day-to-day work on-site. It wasn't until the top clients and then the most talented consultants headed for the door, that the burning in the partners' pockets finally forced them to stop looking after their own turf and to share the load (and the big picture).

look left, look right

A sure sign of poor teamwork across boundaries is that people (including the end customer) are regularly getting surprises from other teams and departments.

Contrast this with a one team culture where there are few surprises because the lines of communication are open and people have an awareness of the impact that their work has on others 'along the line'.

A great way to encourage 'along the line' teamwork is to get people to look at and experience things from the end customer's perspective. With that view they can understand why getting everyone along the value chain to 'look left' and 'look right' is a powerful habit that reduces surprises and creates exceptional results.

This doesn't happen by accident and is usually based on a mindset and culture of equality between areas, rather than competition for status.

'Look left, look right' means recognising that everyone in the value chain shares the same end customer and is equally important in delivering value to that customer. With that in mind, the next step is to be crystal clear about your expectations of those to your left and right.

You will see as the O'Donnell's story unfolds how defining and continually clarifying expectations across the boundaries is a crucial think one team practice.

Look after your own turf |———| *Share the load*

The flip chart marks were again well to the left, but everyone agreed that 'share the load' was much better inside the smaller work teams and departments than across O'Donnell's.

It was a fair point, and O'Donnell's was certainly not alone in that regard, but Sam and Eddie's surfing safari to Coogee Beach was not a good sign. In addition, everyone's pet hate, the almost compulsory late start to meetings while waiting for colleagues to amble in was yet another indication that O'Donnell's had a long way to go to genuinely share the load.

Five practices to defeat 'Three Kingdoms' thinking

Think silos	Think one team
1 Pursue other agendas	1 Share the big picture
2 Avoid and deny	2 Share the reality
3 Stifle communication	3 Share the air
4 Look after your own turf	4 Share the load
5	5

share the wins and losses or play I win, you lose?

The final think one team practice had been a feature of O'Donnell's culture since William and Walter shared a quiet drink with their employees every Friday evening to thank them for their efforts and to share the stories of the week.

In those days O'Donnell's really was one big team and everyone shared the wins and losses.

People still share stories but more typical was last Friday's performance at one of the local bars by Jerry Porter, Deputy Sales Manager and known to all as 'Hippo' on account of his thick skin, huge body and ability to drink more than most of the sales team combined.

As had become the habit on most Friday evenings, the people of O'Donnell's could be found drinking in their own department teams in any of the four bars within walking distance of the plant.

At the nearest of these drinking holes, Hippo was holding court with the sales team, while off in the far corner the finance team mostly sipped glasses of chardonnay, in contrast to Hippo's preferred strategy of one pint of beer in the hand and another waiting on the bar.

With a mouth full of beer nuts Hippo began his story in the loudest voice imaginable while the eight members of the sales team perched on their bar stools eager to hear the latest gossip.

'You need to keep this quiet', he bellowed, completely unaware of anything or anyone around him. 'But our little Jimmy the Sprocket (Jimmy Goh, Sales Manager, to others) is fishing for Grisho's head, and I reckon he might just have hooked up', he announced to more than a few blank looks.

Hippo sensed that more detail might be needed. 'Our illustrious head of Corporate Services and his merry bunch of bean counters have a problem with the budget and they are going to get toasted at next week's board meeting.'

He leaned in towards to the circle of drinkers as if to share a secret, but without dropping the volume one decibel he announced, 'R&D are a hundred grand over budget already, we're two hundred over and you can only guess what Operations are costing us with all their product screw-ups'. Hippo leaned back dangerously on his bar stool and laughed in a snorting fashion that flushed his already red face, still windburned from Wednesday's corporate golf day to which he had scammed an invitation from a mate.

The wine glasses sat untouched as the finance team (and the rest of the bar) listened to Hippo's continuing exposé on the weaknesses, failure and likely demise of all of them. On his fourth pint in thirty minutes and with a fifth waiting on the bar, Hippo was warming to his task as the finance team filed out, leaving Hippo with the last words, 'Those chardonnay bastards will spread our conversation all over the plant by Monday. You can't trust 'em. They're the enemy, just remember that', he advised solemnly as he reached for beer number five.

'A gallon on Friday and you're set for the weekend', Hippo always advised his team. He was halfway to his target as the conversation switched to football and the all-important footy pool.

Play I win, you lose |——————| Share the wins and losses

In the boardroom Tracey from Sales marked the far left of the flip chart and wryly observed, 'It's like that golf saying, "every shot pleases someone". We've become a business in which people take pleasure in watching others fail. It's crazy'.

Jenny was pleased to hear Tracey more engaged in the business than seemed the case at the time of the overheard airport lounge conversation.

O'Donnell's had lost the ability to share the results of its collective efforts and instead had become a 'keep your head down' culture in which any mistakes had to be blamed on someone. 'I win, you lose' thinking was rife, particularly at across-the-business meetings such as the dreaded monthly Sales–Operations forum, where seeing someone else get nailed was actually a relief because it meant you were probably safe for another month.

it's all about end to end

Toyota and a dozen other automobile makers discovered it years ago.

When people can see from the start to the finish of the process they take a lot more care in their part of the action.

Just as a good hockey team links together from defence to attack, so do strong companies think and act 'end to end'.

Take a good look at your business and ask whether silo thinking is stopping people from seeing end to end.

Nick spoke as he added the final practice to the whiteboard. 'In silos no-one sees the overall outcome and they don't share it. Instead of thinking about the business from end to end, they just look at their turf and breathe contentedly when they meet their own KPIs. They compete for resources, for attention and come to see things as win–lose.'

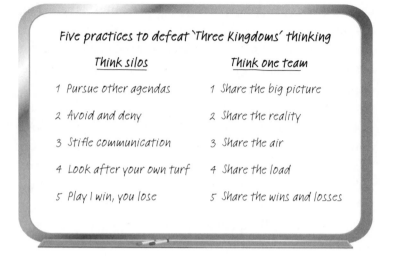

Five practices to defeat 'Three Kingdoms' thinking

Think silos	Think one team
1 Pursue other agendas	1 Share the big picture
2 Avoid and deny	2 Share the reality
3 Stifle communication	3 Share the air
4 Look after your own turf	4 Share the load
5 Play I win, you lose	5 Share the wins and losses

simple and sustainable

Jenny was thrilled with the rapport that Nick had built with the group and was eager to agree to the next steps, particularly what had to be done at tomorrow's staff meeting.

'How do you recommend we move forward Nick?' she asked with unmistakable urgency.

Nick had reached this stage many times with management teams and his pitch was well rehearsed.

'Whatever you do it's got to be simple and sustainable at every level of the company.' He paused for effect and said it again, 'Simple and sustainable at every level of the company'.

Nick replied to Jenny's question.

'From my experience, there are four key steps and they should each run to a tight time frame so we create urgency.

'First, we get a group of leaders all on the same page about think one team and what that specifically means for O'Donnell's. We can do that in a two-day intensive workshop and it will give us a team of coaches who can lay the groundwork for getting everyone else involved.

'Second, the executive team has to create and share the big picture. That means preparing and sending a crystal-clear message about how O'Donnell's will go to market for the next twelve months and beyond.

'Third, every leader from team leader to chief executive has to be coached in how to move from agenda-based leadership to united leadership.'

it's an O'Donnell's bus or nothing

Jim Collins in *Good to Great* used the metaphor of getting the right people on the bus and in the right seats to highlight just how vital it is to get the best people into an organisation and into the roles where they can play to their strengths.[1]

O'Donnell's largely has the right people (Hippo and Mike excluded for now!), but the real problem is that most people have become too comfortable running their own departmental bus companies and no-one is actually on an O'Donnell's bus.

The big challenge for the leadership group is to get people excited so they get off their individual buses and become a part of the journey (the big picture).

[1] J Collins, *Good to Great*, HarperCollins Publishers, New York, 2001.

Nick handed out a small card that looked like this:

Agenda-based leaders:	**United leaders:**
• play politics and refuse to follow an agreed code of behaviour	• hold themselves and their colleagues to standards of behaviour (based on agreed values)
• talk about colleagues' weaknesses and create divisiveness	• talk about colleagues' strengths and see value in diversity
• hide their intentions — keep people at a distance	• show vulnerability and strength by being open
• avoid tough conversations or play the personality not the issue	• have the tough conversation
• debate endlessly	• make decisions and move on
• hold to their own leadership philosophy.	• share and protect the united leadership philosophy.

Nick would explain more about united leadership later because it would be the make or break of think one team in O'Donnell's.

He finished with the fourth and final step — cascading a series of workshops, common tools, problem-solving 'work-outs' and coaching to engage everyone at O'Donnell's in a new and better way of working together.

These four steps would each be important, but none could happen until Jenny O'Donnell made her first and most important presentation to the people of O'Donnell's Jelly Bean Company.

chapter 4

quick wins

It was 4 pm on Thursday and O'Donnell's staff had been arriving at the canteen for the past fifteen minutes.

Mingling in familiar groups and sharing bits of gossip there were even a few bets taken about what Jenny O'Donnell would say. The smart money was on the double of Charles being sacked and some serious redundancy pain.

know how and know why

An American businessman once told me that in his business there was 'plenty of know how and not enough know why'.

Big teams never flourish unless everyone knows the answers to three questions:

1 Where are we heading?

2 Why is that the right direction for the company and for me?

3 How can I play a meaningful part?

Charles believed, as many leaders do, that people only needed to know enough to do their daily tasks. Anything else was unnecessary and, in Charles's view, more likely to distract them from doing their job.

That is dumb management and makes about as much sense as not telling the defenders in a football team that a goal has been scored, or keeping actors in the dark about the overall plot and just leaving them to play their part in isolation.

Jenny knew that the future of O'Donnell's depended on having everyone pulling in the same direction, so she intended to ensure that every staff member knew exactly what was important, why it was important and what their part was in the overall game.

People squeezed into every spare space in the canteen as Jenny stood alongside a lectern and warmly welcomed them and thanked them for coming.

Two cards rested on the lectern, each covered in Jenny's classical-style handwriting.

- *Be clear about your intentions*
- *Act decisively with courage*
- *Give and expect respect*

O'Donnell's Jelly Bean Company values

- *Integrity — with ethics, clear intention and discipline*
- *Passion — tackle everything with energy, commitment and fun*
- *Teamwork — share together, work together and win together*

William would be proud to know that Jenny was bringing O'Donnell's back to its roots.

For half an hour there was not a murmur as Jenny painted the story of O'Donnell's from the earliest days in the kitchen in Birchmore Street to where it was today. More than one long-serving employee wiped away a tear as Jenny described what O'Donnell's meant to her father and uncle, and how William had brought her up to live by the three principles that framed her speech today. It was a deeply personal presentation that connected with people.

'O'Donnell's is not the business we once were, and we are not the business that we want to be. The reality is that we have lost customers and profitability, but more importantly, we have lost our passion for the business and the way we do business.'

She paused and looked out at the sea of receptive faces.

'We used to be a team. We worked together, we played together and we succeeded together.

'It is my intention, with your help, to lead O'Donnell's back to a position where we and our customers know that they are dealing with the best team in the business.'

Applause erupted across the canteen, and even the Hippo was moved to clap and nod his approval.

'That started as of yesterday when the board asked for and received the resignation of the Chief Executive Officer.'

'Plutoed!' exclaimed a loud voice from near the back, as cheering broke out across the canteen and the winners of the bets, including the owner of the loud voice, started plotting how to spend their spoils. 'Plutoed' referred sarcastically to the fate suffered by the planet Pluto when it was summarily removed from the list of planets in the solar system. Charles and Pluto shared a common fate.

Jenny wished that it hadn't come to this and made sure to remain impassive until the noise finally died away.

She wondered what the response might be to her next statement.

'I am now the Chief Executive and will remain so for as long as the board sees that I am the best person to lead this great company.'

More applause reassured her that at least for the time being, this was a move that would galvanise most of O'Donnell's workforce.

She glanced briefly at the card with the line 'Act decisively with courage' on it before continuing.

'I am not going to go into great detail about why Charles was asked to resign because that is unnecessary. I will simply say that at this stage in our history we need a different leadership style and therefore the decision has been made.'

Jenny dropped her voice slightly and spoke in a more measured business-like tone, 'There will be more changes and some pain because there are realities about this business that are not nice. Despite the short-term financial issues, I am convinced that this business has stalled because of our culture, not because of the balance sheet or our products.

'There are people in this room who think the competition is inside the business and who are more interested in their own agendas than O'Donnell's. If that's you, then you have very little time in which to change or you will be leaving.'

Her extended pause gave the line even greater effect. She meant it and no-one in the room doubted her determination to see it through.

'We can and must think and act as one team. We must stop thinking and acting in silos and start using our networks and relationships to our advantage. Therefore, from tomorrow,' she gestured in Nick's direction, 'with the help of Nick Fox and his team, we begin the journey to create a culture in which everyone is committed to think one team'.

Jenny explained that a team of executives, managers and team leaders from across the business would be selected to attend a pilot workshop to experience the think one team concepts and tools. They would then gather data and information from everyone about what was really happening in O'Donnell's before helping to design and facilitate activities in which everyone would be involved. She stressed that this was only the first step in a journey in which everyone would play a vital part.

Jenny took a few questions before again thanking everyone and closing the meeting.

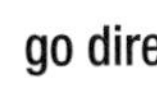

go direct

To generate real one team momentum, bring people together physically.

These cross-functional forums (where a significant proportion of the whole team come together) give the leaders that crucial opportunity to paint a clear, vivid and inspiring big picture.

O'Donnell's got just about everyone into one meeting. In bigger outfits you have to go for a number of meetings. It's like the generals of ancient armies who rode among their people, inspiring them to feel a part of something bigger.

Because Jenny went direct to her people, O'Donnell's now had an appetite for change that wouldn't have happened if she had left it to her lieutenants to pass on the message.

'Go direct' isn't just about team meetings—it also reminds us that having the conversation directly with the right people is essential to breaking down the barriers to communication that flourish in the corporate world.

As people shuffled out of the canteen there was a new mood at O'Donnell's. Nick sensed it and so did Jimmy Goh. He was definitely staying, if Jenny still wanted him.

chapter 5

united leadership

The Lollies on Parade! crisis reminded O'Donnell's that the company could still move fast when the need arose, so by the Monday after Jenny's presentation everything was ready for the workshop.

Facilitated by Nick Fox and his colleague Jess McLeay, the attendees were a cross-section of executives, managers, team leaders and technical specialists. This team of twenty people was the first of many teams that would form across the business as the five practices became a part of the fabric of O'Donnell's.

For two days the participants learned the language and united leadership practices that would transform O'Donnell's from 'think silos' to 'think one team'. They were constantly reminded that leaders must bring the spirit of working as one team—not just the rhetoric or theory—if they are going to inspire people to cross the boundaries.

Around the room you could hear the language—'big picture', 'reality', 'share the air', 'share the workload' and 'win together'.

Under the pressure of a challenging but fun business game the participants surprisingly found themselves pursuing their own agendas, avoiding reality and playing I win, you lose. Old habits die hard.

The two intensive days focused on the theme of united leadership, and were dominated by four topics.

As part of the first topic, titled 'think one team model', the attendees discussed the upsides and downsides of silo thinking and then addressed the realities of silos versus teamwork across boundaries in O'Donnell's. Everything was kept grounded and practical by the question that was pinned near the projection screen: 'What exactly does "think one team" mean for O'Donnell's Jelly Bean Company and what value can it deliver?'

The second topic, 'Capturing the possibilities', brought small teams together to use problem-solving tools to tackle issues identified in the previous session. It was the first taste of cross-functional problem solving using a common language and approach, and during the debriefing a commitment to use the tools in Sales and Operations meetings showed that progress was definitely happening.

In the third topic, 'Establishing partnering relationships', leaders of business units came face-to-face in a challenging exercise to understand each other's hot buttons and define their expectations of each other. Jess and Nick paused occasionally to encourage people to bring a sharper reality to their conversations and to listen first.

The final topic, 'Active coaching', gave each person the confidence and the practical tools that they would need to act as sponsors, supporters and facilitators for the many teams that would be implementing the think one team practices over the coming weeks and months. They were also briefed on their assignments over the next four weeks, which would focus on collecting data and information about one team practices in O'Donnell's.

An exhausted yet inspired group emerged from the workshop with a clear vision of how teamwork across boundaries would be a key to bringing O'Donnell's back to market leadership.

In some ways the workshop was the easy part. The hardest part would be to get people to step off their buses and share the reality of what O'Donnell's had become.

the glue

Think one team is a 'mental model' or a philosophy, not a structure. You can't make it compulsory, but if you want a high-performing organisation, it can't be optional either.

Mental models shape our behaviour, which in turn influence our relationships and then affect what we achieve.

As Mike has already shown, when you have a mental model of pursue your own agenda, then you act in your own best interests, which demolishes trust and collaboration, and you get disasters like Lollies on Parade!

The five think one team practices are the right mental model, but they need a glue to hold them together. That glue is united leadership and it has to come from day-to-day leader behaviour and coaching at every level of the organisation.

Without that glue the wheels will come unstuck under pressure.

stop, start, continue

A group of the coaches devoted a third of their time for the next four weeks to The Big Jelly Bean Team project and met twice weekly as a full group for ninety minutes to debrief, collate their findings and plan the next stage. A training room was converted into project headquarters. Judith Corrigan, the Human Resources Executive, was the Project Coordinator and Jess McLeay acted as the Implementation Facilitator. The headquarters became a hub of activity and a place to review data, share ideas and maintain the momentum.

Using online questionnaires and checklists provided by Nick, the coaches launched a blitz of interviews, focus groups, surveys and the all-important chats in corridors to extract a total picture of what was really happening in O'Donnell's.

They operated in pairs and worked half of the time in their own area of the business and the other half in a different area. This ensured that employees dealt with someone they knew but also that fresh eyes looked over each area.

Their brief was to create a current-state map of the business, based on the five rules and addressing three key questions:

- What must we stop doing?
- What must we start doing?
- What must we continue doing?

	stop	start	continue
share the big picture			
share the reality			
share the air			
share the load			
share the wins and losses			

share the reality

Inside the project room the coaches poured over information that was coming in from the questionnaires.

'Look at the Sales division ratings', remarked Donna Smart, pointing at a partnering scorecard graph that showed a business unit in which people neither thought end to end nor looked left and right.

'It'll be interesting to correlate this with the leadership scorecard', commented Max, the Business Analyst, who was having a ball analysing the data. He flicked to a new screen and shook his head as Hippo's 360-degree feedback profile showed red-line performance in every key direction.

I value your opinion . . . but show me the data

One of my colleagues saw the saying, 'I value your opinion . . . but show me the data' on a wall in a top international manufacturing business. It's a great way to remind everyone to go past people's individual opinions and instead get accurate information or feedback before turning the place upside down. This applies equally to a think one team initiative as to any other business change.

Begin by measuring against the five practices so you know how and where agendas prevail and whether people are teaming effectively.

The next step is to benchmark and monitor the quality of relationships and delivery across key boundaries. This allows you to intervene before the delivery falls apart.

Finally, measure the united leadership practices.

Remember—I value your opinion on the teamwork and partnering in your business . . . but show me the data.

The data from all the questionnaires would be used by the facilitators in the workshops that would follow the initial data-collection phase.

For Mike, it would be one of his first share-the-reality experiences, as one of O'Donnell's major destroyers of team-work came face to face with the impact of his behaviour.

It would also be the first and badly needed dose of reality for some O'Donnell's employees and teams who had hidden behind their own agendas for too long.

big picture

While most of the coaches worked on creating a clear map of the reality inside the business, members of the executive team used the model that Steve Edwards had run through on the day that Charles was fired to look at the competitive position of the business.

Jenny wanted to be armed with this information to go to the board, the executive and the whole organisation with one big picture of the reality of O'Donnell's and it's potential. The time frame was tight but the size of O'Donnell's and the commitment of Jenny and the coaches made it possible.

a snapshot

Among all the details gathered by the coaches, three examples typified the issues facing Jenny and the whole O'Donnell's business.

simplicity wins

It's not a word that you'll find in *The Australian Oxford Dictionary* but 'dumbplexity' seems to sum-up how organisations have a habit of adding unnecessary and dumb complexity when what they really need is smart simplicity.

Rodney Williams from R&D and Andrew Ireland from Sales had applied the principle 'think end to end' to create a process map of how information from customers finds its way back through the business. They were now looking at how quickly and effectively complaints, ideas and compliments found their way through the business.

'Have you heard the story about the interviewer who asked the train-wreck question?' asked Rodney as he was collating information from a group meeting they had co-facilitated.

Andrew was absorbed in calculating average response times to customer complaints. 'No,' he replied, 'what's that one?'

Rodney explained, 'There's this guy who works for the railways and he applies for a management job. At the interview he is given this scenario:

> You are staying with your family at a country hotel and decide to go for a walk along a high ridge from where you can see for kilometres in all directions. From there you see two passenger trains heading towards each other on the same line: neither can see the other. You're curious, so you look through your binoculars at the trains and then at the signal at the fork in the line. You realise from experience that the lines are not switched for the trains to bypass each other and therefore a crash will happen in about five minutes. You have a mobile phone so what do you do?

Andrew had stopped checking the numbers and waited for Rodney to continue.

> The applicant just smiles confidently and says, 'I'd call the railway's emergency number and get put through to central traffic control and get them to electronically flip the switch'.

'Fine,' says the interviewer, 'but the railway's phone system takes thirty seconds to run through the options like "press one" to change your tickets and so on, and there isn't a number to prevent train wrecks so you're in a queue that could take up to ten minutes. Even if you then get through, the railways have such a long line of command that it will take up to a day to get the okay to change the signal. By that time the trains will have crashed'.

'Okay,' says the applicant, slightly shaken, 'then I'd run down the hill and manually change the signal myself because I know how the system works'.

'Sorry,' replies the interviewer, 'but a new system has been installed by the railway's IT Department and it doesn't have a manual override because it is guaranteed failsafe'.

'Alright,' says the now-exasperated applicant, 'then I'd call Emergency Services and get them to contact the trains directly and also to send ambulances in case the trains do crash'.

'That would have worked,' explains the interviewer, 'except that the Emergency Services communication centre is actually run by a telecommunications company who have outsourced their call centre to overseas. When you report that the trains are in Gladstone the courteous gentleman with the foreign accent wastes valuable time before realising he has entered the wrong Gladstone into the computer. You, and more importantly the trains, are in a different state.'

'So, what do you do now?' the interviewer asks, confident that he'd completely thrown the bewildered applicant.

'I'd dash back to the hotel and get my son, Ben', replied the applicant. 'Does he know something about trains?' enquires the slightly confused interviewer.

'No,' replied applicant, 'but he's never seen a train crash!'

Andrew and Rodney laughed together.

'That's O'Donnell's customer service system isn't it?' said Rodney, banging the table to emphasise the point.

'Yeah, from what we've gathered, the IT guys have managed to create a system that is almost impregnable to customer complaints. We could be sugarising rat poison and even half a million people ringing to complain would be lucky to get past the phone queue to our two customer service people.'

'And if they did,' added Andrew, 'their complaint would be painstakingly recorded on the complaints form, which is emailed automatically to the Customer Service Coordinator, who reviews it within a week and then raises it at the customer service meeting that was last held four months ago'.

'And when a really pissed off customer complains to the Sales guys we have to fill out the same form, which takes thirty minutes to complete and has to be keyed into the system because customer service won't deal with internal phone calls.'

Rodney and Andrew had uncovered just one of the many processes in O'Donnell's that had become so complex that it had lost the point of why it was created in the first place. Dumbplexity must be thrown out or teamwork will be smothered by unnecessary rules and processes.

Einstein was right... as usual!

While Albert Einstein once said, 'Things should be made as simple as possible, but not any simpler', it seems that many businesses prefer the motto, 'Make everything as complex as possible, and no less so'.

Create a medium-sized organisation, get really busy and keep the people who are responsible for technology as far away from the end user(s) as possible and you have the ideal conditions for this sort of dumbplexity to flourish.

The cure for dumbplexity is simplicity, and every business needs some 'simplicity evangelists' who seek and destroy technology and/or processes that serve something other than their purpose.

Customers are the ideal simplicity evangelists because they are too often on the end of something that a head office genius has created for 'administrative ease' or to save costs.

Vote with your feet when you experience dumbplexity as a customer, and ruthlessly drive it out when you find it in your business. Take Einstein's advice to make it as simple as possible, but no more so because simplicity wins.

who's the competition?

Silos don't just operate vertically as Sarah Nuyen and Ed Gergiou discovered on hearing story after story of the way the senior managers in O'Donnell's keep secrets.

In the past year, three project teams had continued working on projects for up to two months after the executive team canned the project. No-one thought to tell the people who were actually doing the work!

'How can that happen?' asked Sarah, a Finance Accountant (and chardonnay drinker), of two technologists from R&D. 'Simple', replied one of the chemists. 'Emma was on long service leave and when an executive is away there isn't a proxy sent to their meetings. It was only when she came back and heard about the decision that we were pulled off the job. It's typical of the exec club.'

The reference to 'the exec club' made Sarah recall how Ron always came in from leave to attend the fortnightly executive meeting.

'I'd always thought it was Ron Grisham who kept everything secret about exec meetings,' commented Sarah, 'but maybe there's more to it than that'.

Ed, the Quality Systems Manager, felt compelled to add his thoughts. 'I've only been here six months but since Steve Edwards arrived he's always given us a briefing on anything from exec that's relevant to our operations.'

'Well, that's good for you,' countered Klaus the older of the two food technologists, 'but I think if you ask people right down the line you'll find that O'Donnell's is set up like a building with solid floors between levels and walls between departments. Steve might be the exception, but I think you'll find that there are massive blockages at team-leader level right across the business'.

Half an hour later and Klaus had recounted story after story of competition between team leaders. There was competition for resources, for attention, for promotion and for just being in control.

'How do you think Smithy was promoted from IT to Customer Service?' he asked.

Sarah shrugged.

'He was recommended by his boss because it was the only way to get the incompetent turkey out of IT', replied Klaus with a smirk. 'There's at least half-a-dozen people in this company who just get shuffled from one place to another because no-one's honest enough to say they're not up to it. Team leaders just flick their problems to someone else.'

Sarah and Ed relayed the conversation and their reflections at their next project meeting. Many of the coaches shared similar stories and noted that the data from the questionnaires was showing that poor teamwork across boundaries wasn't just between departments, but also between levels of the hierarchy.

'To respond faster and better than other organisations,' explained Nick to the coaches, 'you must be networked in a way that fosters communication from executive to team leaders to staff and back again. From what I can see, O'Donnell's has a culture in which people get their power and importance from holding onto information. That's a disaster because it sets up competition and slows everything down.'

Jenny nodded. 'There is no doubt that one of my first jobs is to close down the executive club and start trusting our employees with the information they need to make us all successful.'

The Big Jelly Bean Team project was on track and Nick could already see the whole place was starting to think and act more like one team instead of competing against each other.

playing the blame game

Despite people being reluctant to openly criticise Mike due to his close relationship with both Charles and the previous head of Operations, the coaches quickly uncovered the games he had been playing.

The extreme scores on the questionnaires ensured he was invited to meet with Nick and Jenny soon after the results were in. They were horrified when checking Mike's previous performance management reports to find that he had been rated by his manager as 'high' in every category.

O'Donnell's, like many organisations, avoided tackling poor performance, but it began today with a very clear understanding between Mike and Jenny that he would improve all aspects of his contribution to teamwork or leave the business.

An angry Mike returned to his department and over the next hour confronted three of his colleagues about whether they had given him bad feedback in the questionnaires. Not surprisingly, he didn't tell them that he had tossed blame in their direction and he fully expected them to get the same carpeting as him.

Mike was an expert at the blame game but it's a game that is hard to play as the organisation opens the doors and windows of the silos and frees up communication. The team leaders had been coached in a feedback tool aptly called 'REAL', so they decided that a REAL conversation with Mike was in order.

Just before 4 pm Mike, his three colleagues and Jenny met for what descended into a bitter exchange as Mike dished out dirt and threats to all and sundry. His performance was way below the 'low bar' on the value of 'give and expect respect'.

Jenny knew all about industrial law and the risks of legal action, however, she was convinced that Mike had to go for the benefit of the whole team.

It was a 'best for the business' decision and he was gone within the hour, still blaming others and threatening legal action.

find the truth

I read once that in any difficult situation the person who can best describe the truth without blame will emerge as the leader.

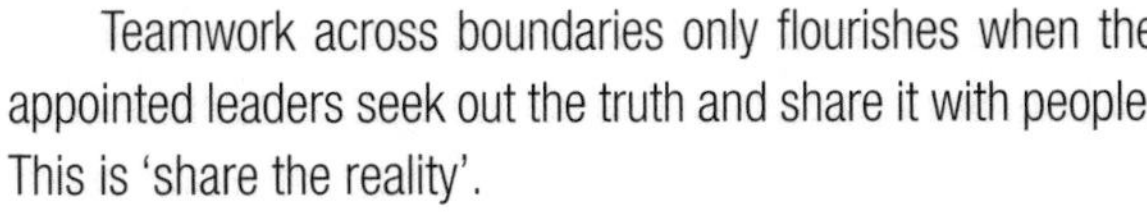

Teamwork across boundaries only flourishes when the appointed leaders seek out the truth and share it with people. This is 'share the reality'.

In Mike's case, the truth was that he didn't want to be part of one team and his behaviour reinforced the old way of doing business that Charles had epitomised.

In some situations you may have enough time and resources to try to bring Mike onboard, but the future of O'Donnell's was at risk, therefore the sooner Jenny confronted that truth and got Mike out the better for everyone—even Mike in the longer term.

How leaders at all levels handle the Mikes of this world says a lot about their commitment to the big picture, to sharing the reality and sharing the load.

Removing Mike had an even greater short-term effect on the morale of the workforce than Charles's demise because most people knew of his game playing and saw Jenny's decision as a clear signal that this think one team stuff was here to stay. And most were delighted.

chapter 6

sharing the big picture

After four weeks of intensive activity the members of The Big Jelly Bean Team Project met together for a full day to share their findings and recommendations on how best to move forward.

To make sure that every attendee had a complete understanding of the reality of O'Donnell's position and potential, Jenny opened the day by presenting four of the points from the impromptu presentation that Steve Edwards had given to the executive a few weeks ago.

On the projection screen a third column had been added to Steve's original work and it was there that everyone's attention hung.

Where we came from	**Sharing the reality**	**The big picture ... our future**
Customers will buy the best jelly beans in the world	Customers are buying other products instead of ours	*Think like a customer*
Profits come from having a great product	We are unprofitable	*Think like a business owner*
Don't change the O'Donnell's business model	Our business model is broken	*Think like a leader*
Make teams accountable for their own performance	We are many teams not one team	*Think one team*

Like the words in the third column, Jenny's presentation was short, sharp and to the point.

No-one was left in any doubt that the big picture for O'Donnell's, while still about making the world's best jelly beans, was also about a different way of connecting with customers, about shifting from an employee to a business-owner mindset, about leadership at every level of the company and replacing the silos with the five practices of think one team.

Jenny concluded with a call to action. 'We have a choice here and it's not one that I can make alone. We can choose to set the bar low and maybe scrape through this current problem with a few casualties. And perhaps that's a comfortable thing to do for some of you. Sometimes it is easier to just accept your conditions and learn to put up with them.'

challenge the status quo

Unleashing the power of one team sounds sexy, but it hits hard against the status quo in most organisations.

Why? There are lots of reasons, but some of the usual suspects include that people have clearly marked their power bases and comfort zones, which means that one way or another they dodge reality.

Jenny is challenging the status quo by staking out a new playing field:

- *Think like a customer* means putting customers first—not managers and employees—when planning for products and services. For example, in O'Donnell's this means realigning the business to suit customers who want variety not just one colour.
- *Think like a business owner* means that everyone understands the big picture, the current performance and how their efforts are helping or hindering.
- *Think like a leader* means shaping the future instead of reacting to, or even resisting, change.

These messages are basic and they work under pressure because they set up the foundation for everyone to think one team.

She looked around the room at the sea of faces. Each with their own thoughts. Each with their own hopes and concerns.

'I know that most of you want more than just a job. You want a future. You want to be part of a winning team, not one that's scraping by on the strength of a fading brand name.

'Sure we can cut costs and probably hold onto a patch of the market, but who wants to live their life just surviving?

'Fortunately, we have a second choice. We can refuse to contemplate being a victim of our circumstances. We can use all the strengths in our products, our brand and our people to lay out a bigger picture in which O'Donnell's is the market leader in the areas we choose to compete in.

'And that's where we're going; however, as we work through the issues today I want everyone to recognise that this isn't simply a question of do you or don't you want to be a part of the business. It's a question of "Are we prepared to change everything, including ourselves, to make that vision real?"'

There was a mood of resolute optimism in the room as this team of united leaders began what was most definitely a share-the-reality presentation.

it's about attitude

'We need to make some big changes', Tracey, one of the sales team leaders, explained, 'but they don't have to be hugely complex or expensive because mostly they're about the attitudes and behaviour of all of us'.

'Simple and sustainable', thought Steve as Tracey continued.

She flicked on a slide and pointed to the list that appeared on the projection screen:

- Share the big picture
- Share the reality
- Share the air
- Share the load
- Share the wins and losses

'It's about doing these five things brilliantly and we're well underway because these past four weeks have already shown how much we can achieve when we share the reality and share the air.'

Each member of the project team shared the mix of stories and data that they had collected over the four weeks. Time and again their stories of successful projects and performance revealed what happened when O'Donnell's people worked across the boundaries, shared a common big picture and brought the five practices to life. In contrast, there were many examples of agendas, blame, stifled communication and turf fights that inevitably ended poorly for O'Donnell's and its customers. Each presenter related what he or she had found to the five practices, and showed a strong commitment to opening the doors and windows of the silos.

'Excellent', exclaimed Nick, eager not to lose the positive momentum that was building. 'We have three things to do: first, get ready to present to everyone in the company, second, confirm the big picture and, third, map out how we want the think one team wave to wash over the company.'

find solutions, not blame

All O'Donnell's staff attended think one team workshops timed to allow for production to continue without major interruption.

The first set of workshops were large group activities designed to explain and make the link between the company's future direction and think one team, and to give people a deeper understanding of the core tools and practices that would be implemented across the business. Perhaps the biggest challenge was shaking the complacency that had descended on the business. Inevitably, that would touch some raw nerves but Nick insisted that everyone in the business be 'on the same page' and that meant giving them the big picture, warts and all.

The second set of workshops were conducted as 'work-outs' in which two or more teams came together over two days to develop partnering agreements, tackle joint problems and identify ways to open the doors and windows of the silos.

All workshops were designed and co-facilitated by the coaches and a member of Nick's team. Using O'Donnell's coaches showed management's commitment to the program and the resulting implementation plan for the first three months ensured that everyone made the connection between the workshops and day-to-day business.

The only ground rule for coaches was that when negative things about O'Donnell's and its people were raised, the process had to be facilitated in a constructive way that finished by looking forward. It was a tactic that Nick had learned from a sport psychologist who observed that the best coaches hold really tough conversations, but they leave their athletes looking forward (instead of still looking to blame or rationalise).

'We have many harsh realities to share in the coming months,' Nick stressed, 'but that won't improve the business unless people see the leaders focusing on solutions instead of blame'.

the first think one team workshop

The first of the opening set of workshops was held at a nearby conference centre and began with a team game designed to challenge people to work in small teams while striving towards an overall big picture. The game was like a combination of three-dimensional jigsaw puzzles and pass-the-parcel, and, amidst mayhem and laughter, showed everyone what happens when people think small teams instead of one team.

After debriefing the game and linking it to the five practices the attendees were prepared for the main activity of the day.

Workstations had been set up around the room and labelled according to the five practices, starting from the left with 'Share the big picture' and moving around to 'Share the wins and losses'. At each station, data and information collected by the coaches was displayed in easy-to-understand formats on posters.

For the next few hours groups were shuffled around under the guidance of Nick and Jess until by mid-afternoon flip-chart paper covered the walls. Items were recorded in coloured pen under the headings 'Stop', 'Start', 'Continue'. Stars next to some items identified them as the 'big bang' items to give attention.

Three members of the project team, Donna, Max and Jenny, stood back from the 'Share the big picture' work-station as staff milled around posters debating issues, jotting ideas on flip charts and moving on as they were ready to engage with another group.

'Are we getting to the big issues?' asked Jenny of her two bright and enthusiastic colleagues.

In the 'Stop' column three items had stars next to them:

Stop

- ☆ *using department goals and measures that set up internal competition*
- ☆ *making decisions without consulting the people who are affected*
- ☆ *the management clubs (exec and team leaders)*

'They're pretty much what I would expect', said Max, looking further down the column at some of the other 'stops'.

Stop
• *the 'cyb' emails*
• *the personality feuds between Sales and Finance*
• *refusing to take a customer call*

Jess and Nick conferred as people mixed, chatted, challenged, laughed, debated and did everything that you would expect of people who were on the same team.

'It's building a head of steam', Jess observed as a burst of applause rose from a group near the 'Share the load' wall.

'What's that one all about?' asked Nick, his view of the poster obscured by Nathan Smith, the 195 centimetre tall former football star who worked in Operations and won the heart of just about every girl at O'Donnell's.

Jess laughed, 'It says, "Scrap the SLAs"'.

SLA was code for Service Level Agreements, the dreaded contracts between departments that were brought in to improve the in-company customer service, but did nothing more than create demarcation and a weapon for one part of the company to use against the other. IT and Finance copped the worst of it as Sales and Operations demanded that their priorities be met, although more than once the positions were reversed as they were told to wait their turn because 'it isn't in the SLA!'

More cheering arose from the direction of 'Share the wins and losses'.

'STOP GOING TO SEPARATE BARS ON FRIDAYS!!!' was scrawled in capital letters across the poster, and a beaming Hippo burst from the group dancing with an equally animated Sarah, the chardonnay drinker from Finance.

'Yes, yes, yes', chanted three members of the sales team as 'Start getting Finance to work with Sales to monitor the budgets' was logged as an action in 'Share the wins and losses'.

scrap the SLAs

If you need a formal service-level contract between two or more departments or functions, I'd respectfully suggest that you sack the managers of those areas because it is they who are accountable for aligning expectations, delivering on commitments and keeping the lines of communication open.

Too often SLAs reinforce power struggles inside the business, and make collaboration and trust harder to establish.

Scrap the SLAs and replace them with genuine (written) Partnering Agreements backed up by a structured Partnering Plan for the essential linkages or relationships.

Make your relationships with colleagues equal because thinking 'one team' is all about across-the-boundaries teamwork built on trust. That means partnering in both directions and it is why in think one team programs we measure the across-the-boundaries partnering of all key teams and put that on the corporate dashboard.

The energy built as the facilitators skilfully shifted the attention of the whole group backwards and forwards from the big picture to the posters and flip chart in front of them. By late afternoon action lists were refined, priorities agreed and development tasks (with deadlines) allocated to cross-functional teams.

The next day an almost identical workshop with another group of managers and staff showed everyone that O'Donnell's was ready to dump silo thinking and build a new future around the mantra 'think one team'.

chapter 7

a focus on partnering

three months later

Every month Jenny O'Donnell assembled the leaders of O'Donnell's Jelly Bean Company to review progress and set the next month's priorities. Executives and coaches worked as partners without the status barriers and poor listening that had previously stifled communication.

Quick wins built the momentum for change as staff saw that O'Donnell's really could be reinvented without losing the parts of the culture that they all loved.

The workshops and problem-solving work-outs had brought people together, instilled new attitudes and behaviours, and delivered real improvements in productivity and service.

Joe Narella was a breath of fresh air in Customer Service despite the complete disbelief from Judith that Charles had recruited a person sight unseen from the other side of the world.

A reinvigorated Jimmy Goh had the Sales team firing on all cylinders, and for the first time O'Donnell's jelly beans were mixed together in the cellophane bags. Innovative new colours and flavours, product shapes and some stunning promotional ideas showed what happened when R&D and Marketing started thinking as one team and acting as partners.

Steve led the disbandment of the production 'kingdoms' in favour of a more flexible arrangement where people were encouraged and rewarded for moving across different parts of the business. Almost miraculously, the continuous-improvement teams, project-management tools and dreaded performance-management system were actually starting to fulfil their promise, instead of being just more O'Donnell's fads that didn't work.

'Simplicity wins' had become a new catchcry, replacing the 'dumbplexity' that had added to costs and slowed O'Donnell's to a crawl. Accountability for decisions was pushed as far into the business as possible and people became accustomed to being accountable for performance in their own function *and* for creating value across the boundaries.

Finance was producing management information that empowered team leaders to run their operations like small businesses, and under Jenny's leadership the executive opened the lines of communication and started acting like high-performance leaders instead of mediocre managers.

Importantly, O'Donnell's didn't fall into the trap of thinking that teamwork meant making everyone dependent on everyone else. Quite the opposite. Where interdependency was useful they made it work through well-defined partnering agreements, but where it slowed down decision making and customer service it was avoided. It really was 'Silos with holes in them', as Jimmy noted.

Collegiate meetings with tight agendas and a focus on partnering replaced the high-spin, high-blame, cross-functional meetings. Meeting rooms were stocked with posters and toolkits to reinforce the think one team messages of five practices and consistency in problem solving, partnering and debriefing.

Among all the changes, arguably the most telling was the reception area. Susan still smiled, but the Rottweiler had chosen guard duty at another company and those stunning glass cylinders no longer stood as the perfect symbol of the silos in O'Donnell's.

The cylinders themselves remained, but now they were randomly filled with different-coloured beans, which reminded everyone to think one team.

chapter 8

inspiration

six months later, kowloon, hong kong

A Chinese junk bobbed in the wake of a sleek white ferry, the captains briefly exchanging glances as they plied their trade in the auditorium that is Hong Kong harbour. A fluffy white cloud hung over Victoria Peak as if joining Nick Fox in savouring one of the great city views of the world.

As far as views from hotel rooms go, Nick rated the one from the Royal Pacific Hotel in Kowloon one of the best he had seen, but most of the forty or so delegates were more familiar with the view than with the curious set-up of the room that had greeted them on arrival at the conference room that morning.

Expecting the customary training-room format of tables and chairs, they milled uncomfortably in small, tight groups between the workstations around the auditorium's perimeter and the five round tables in the middle of the room that were each adorned with three small glass cylinders full of blue, red and black jelly beans, respectively.

From banks, governments, shipping companies, insurers, miners, fast-moving consumer goods, telecommunications and hospitality businesses they had come to learn about, and experience the power of, big teams.

Hong Kong is proof that businesses no longer make money just from assets, and the nationalities of the attendees made it quite clear that the old boundaries of country, industry and gender were no more. With money flowing at the speed of light and ideas a dime a dozen, the banker from Shanghai, the mining executive from Denver and the IT CEO from Bangalore were there because the only thing their competitors can't buy or copy is the culture of their business, and more specifically the power that comes when everyone thinks one team.

It was now nine months since Nick Fox landed in Australia in search of inspiration that he'd expected to come from his own ideas. But as is so often the case, it was something totally out of left field that delivered more than he could ever have dreamed possible.

He pushed down against the nervous anticipation rising in his stomach and flicked the switch that brought his lapel microphone to life.

'Welcome to the think one team workshop', he announced to the still-standing executives.

On cue, waiters dressed in crisp white jackets appeared from every entrance of the round conference room, carrying silver trays full of brightly coloured jelly beans. Each tray contained just one colour: red, blue, black or green. Each jelly bean was the size of a bird's egg.

'Please sample one of each colour,' Nick smiled, 'but leave the green to last'. He motioned the four waiters with trays of green jelly beans to the rear of the room, leaving the others in what quickly became a polite, yet eager feeding frenzy.

Nods of approval. Groans of delight. Savouring of the taste explosion that is the O'Donnell's black jelly bean. No sweet anywhere in the world quite matched the O'Donnell's bean at its best.

'Has anyone not yet tasted the blue, red and black jelly beans?' enquired a female voice from the rear of the room. The audience turned towards the sound.

A petite Chinese woman in her mid forties stood flanked by four waiters each with the trays of green beans. Mai Lee, born in Hong Kong of mixed-race parents and educated in London, was one of Nick's best facilitators, with a host of clients across Asia and Europe.

'Please take one green bean and a tissue', she instructed politely.

The waiters pressed forward among the audience followed soon after by howls of disapproval and muffled spitting into the tissues. Cultural differences defined the extent of the reactions.

'Ladies and gentlemen', Nick paused as they shifted attention towards him. 'Over the next two days you will experience the story of the company that made those magnificent blue, red and black jelly beans.'

As waiters again moved through the crowd collecting the green-stained tissues and handing out blue jelly beans to replace the taste of cats' urine being experienced by the audience, Nick continued.

'It is difficult to believe, but that those disgusting green jelly beans were also made by the very same company, using the same people and the same production process.'

the think one team experience

For two days, bankers, miners, insurers and public servants worked together through a series of business simulations, presentations and workshop activities. Workstations around the auditorium became production, sales and purchasing departments, while executives scurried between them. Every few hours a presentation brought O'Donnell's, the jelly bean company from Sydney, to life in the conference room overlooking Hong Kong Harbour.

Facilitated by Nick and Mai Lee, the first part of the opening simulation showed what happened when the first rule of think one team was broken. Instead of 'share the big picture' the subteams of insurers, tourism specialists and government executives played 'pursue your own agenda'.

Building from the scripts provided by the facilitators a hilarious but frighteningly real show played out as one department competed against another. Sales overhyped its forecasts, R&D avoided getting anywhere near a customer, executives emailed everyone about 'the mission and vision' of their departments and IT refused to assist Finance because it was outside the SLA. Groans of recognition from the audience showed how real the scenes were to their businesses.

The second part of the opening simulation brought 'share the big picture' to life. Characters changed. Collaboration replaced competition, executive emails were supplanted by one-on-one conversations and cross-business partnering became a way of life. The scripts provided by Nick and

Mai Lee introduced the tools and techniques that had worked to break down the agendas in O'Donnells.

An intensive debrief followed each performance and then there was time for attendees to focus on their own businesses. Working in small groups they challenged each other about the way that the practices of think one team played out in their businesses.

From the O'Donnell's purchasing debacles they learned how teamwork across boundaries doesn't flourish until you create genuine partnering relationships with shared goals and aligned expectations. In O'Donnell's that meant bringing the Purchasing and Production teams together in a new and well-defined partnership, while for the Mining Executive it will mean creating new relationships and performance metrics so that Mine Production teams and Global Supply Chain work as one team instead of in constant friction.

From O'Donnell's 'spin', they learned how to confront reality and to keep a scorecard that measures delivery and relationships between partners, alongside the more traditional production volumes, inventory and cash on hand. The banker from Shanghai was determined to tear down the reward system that fostered across-the-bank competition and to put in new scorecards that reward what is best for the business. Previously, he might have just issued an order, but now he would bring together a cross-functional team and choose the path of united leadership.

From O'Donnell's willingness to 'share the reality' they learned the power of open conversation and practised having the direct and respectful conversations that are the lifeblood of a one team culture.

Nearing the end of day two, in the final interactive session, there was great cheering as the small department teams lifted the caps from the top of the cylinders of jelly beans, tipped the contents into bowls, mixed them together and then refilled the cylinders.

Like the entrance to O'Donnell's, the cylinders had been the ultimate symbol of silo thinking and poor teamwork. As the executives headed towards the airport, they excitedly planned how to bring the energy and passion of think one team to their businesses. Foremost in their minds was the realisation that from the tables in Hong Kong and the entrance to O'Donnell's offices in Sydney, the multicoloured cylinders revealed that it isn't about big jelly beans, but rather about *being* The Big Jelly Bean Team.

fifteen months later

It was two years ago to the day that Jenny O'Donnell, with a resolve to save her father's legacy, took over the reigns of O'Donnell's Jelly Bean Company. Tonight she sat alone. Her choice of restaurant was more for nostalgia than the cuisine, although Doyles, the famous seafood restaurant at Watsons Bay with the stunning view along Sydney Harbour towards the Opera House, could rate with the best. She was deep in thought as a huge white cruise ship slipped silently past, its wake slapping against the shore.

Lights twinkled along the harbour as they had done years before when Jenny shared her last meal with her father. It had been two days before her thirtieth birthday.

'Jenny,' he had said in the rasping voice of a man with too few breaths left to live, 'as you know there has always been a plaque on the wall in my office with the three principles that I have lived by in my business life for forty years.' He paused to draw breath while tears welled in her eyes. 'I know that these principles are also important to you, however, there is one missing and I only realised it in the past few years, perhaps because I took it for granted.'

Jenny waited as her father coughed a hard, painful cough that would claim his life just five days later. 'When times are tough you need more than intention, courage and respect, you need people to share the highs and lows—to see a bigger picture than you can find by yourself. You need to talk and listen, to be honest with each other and to share the load. Sometimes you find those people in your family or your community or in your business. I'm lucky that I had a great partner in marriage, another in my business and then a big team of partners at O'Donnell's. I like to think of all these people as being just a part of one big team.

'For too long I took those partners for granted and in you I see some of the stubbornness and independence that I came to see in myself. The three principles are wonderful and I hope that you continue to keep them in mind.'

He handed Jenny the plaque with the three principles and she looked at them knowing how much they meant to a dying man.

Be clear about your intentions

Act decisively with courage

Give and expect respect

'There was no space on the front for the fourth principle, so I pencilled it on the back as a reminder.'

Jenny turned over the plaque and written in William's impeccably neat handwriting was the phrase:

think one team

chapter 9

a passion for teamwork across boundaries

It was completely dark outside when Nick Fox spotted Jenny in the far corner of Doyles. She was pushing down the emotions of ten years ago as his 'Hi, Jen' startled her back to the present.

She had intentionally arrived half an hour before Nick. She wanted time to be with her memories so she could then give Nick her full attention to explain why she had approached him to work with O'Donnell's.

They shared a bottle of wine and half chatted, half watched the busy harbour as they caught up on all the little pieces of gossip about O'Donnell's and their common friendships.

Somewhere between the main course and dessert Jenny told Nick about the plaque that her father had given her and the fourth principle that she had never shared with anyone.

In that conversation her father had remarked on a young man who was the son of a legal adviser William had engaged at O'Donnell's. The young man was researching the topic of 'big teams' and he had interviewed William as part of his work. The conversation was the inspiration for the fourth principle, so when he handed over the plaque and mentioned that principle he also spoke about Nick Fox and his passion for big teams.

Jenny had never raised the conversation with Nick in their time working together, but when O'Donnell's was in trouble she decided that the timing of his return to Australia was too great an opportunity not to get him involved.

Since then, not only had Nick's business grown enormously but O'Donnell's Jelly Bean Company had also built rapidly as businesses across Asia and the United States (due in no small part to Nick's workshops) had awakened to the experience of the O'Donnell's jelly bean. Massive orders now meant a large factory in southern China and another soon to open in Mexico. O'Donnell's featured on all the 'hottest businesses' lists, and an imminent public listing would provide the capital needed to keep pace with demand.

Nick reached into his thin black satchel and drew out a book that he placed on the table in front of Jenny.

She burst out laughing at the sight of the brightly coloured cover.

'You did it!' she exclaimed, in a voice loud enough to make diners at the other end of the restaurant look up, as she grasped the cover of *think one team*.

'Isn't it incredible', she observed more quietly after flicking through the book. 'Because of your workshops we are actually making more money out of those disgusting green jelly beans than we ever made from the Sydney factory alone!'

Jenny turned to the last page of the book on which were just three words: **think one team**.

the think one team™ model

It is both natural and desirable for organisations to separate into smaller units such as divisions, departments and teams. This separation gives focus, specialisation and ownership, which offer the promise of greater efficiency and effectiveness, faster decision making and increased enjoyment for the people involved.

Unfortunately, this separation into units often comes at a cost.

Instead of leverage and growth there is a legacy of increased conflict, unnecessary complexity, failure to leverage assets, damaged brands and reduced service.

The challenge, therefore, is to create an organisation that captures both the benefits of focused business units *and* the opportunities that come from effective teamwork and partnering.

There is no simple formula for designing an organisation because everything from strategic direction to information systems, to structure, to work tasks and even geography plays a part. Importantly, however, the'make or break'seems to be less about structure and more about relationships and behaviours. Put simply, we have to be good at task focus and collaborative networking at the same time.

The think one team™ model describes the five practices that characterise organisations (and communities) and create value from the networking of their parts. In a world where businesses want and need both the focus of specialised business units and the value of synergies between those units, the five practices are a simple and powerful model.

The following section contains further detail on the five practices and ideas on how to bring this model to life. Further details, including articles and program outlines, can be viewed at <www.thinkoneteam.com>.

the foundation

From studying and consulting with many different-sized organisations across the business and non-business world, it became clear to me that there were quite distinct differences between the practices of people within unnecessarily siloed organisations and those that acted like one big team.

This experience led to identifying five practices that distinguish these two types of organisations. Each of these practices has an opposite or 'shadow'. For example, 'share the big picture' has as its shadow 'pursue other agendas'.

A brief overview of the five think one team™ practices is outlined overleaf, together with an explanation of their opposite.

think one team	think silos
Share the big picture	Pursue other agendas
Share the reality	Avoid and deny
Share the air	Stifle communication
Share the load	Look after your own turf
Share the wins and losses	Play I win, you lose

1 *Share the big picture* is the first practice, and means that everyone and every team knows and shares their part in the bigger picture. That picture might be of the corporate vision and values, or simply just understanding what is happening in the next department. The shadow, *pursue other agendas,* is characterised by the individual parts of the organisation pursuing other things that are more important than the big picture.

2 *Share the reality* is the second practice, and is about speaking the truth, confronting the harsh reality and being open to giving and receiving feedback. The shadow is *avoid and deny,* and its guises include putting an overly positive 'spin' on issues or avoiding them altogether. When reality is avoided or denied, the whole organisation is at risk.

3 *Share the air* is essential if potential is to be tapped. The lifeblood of organisations is communication. Open two-way communication, active listening and clear communication stops the damaging silos from flourishing. However, when the shadow *stifle communication* is in place, people dominate others

or, alternatively, they hoard information and foster a 'them and us' culture.

4 *Share the load* is the fourth practice, and happens spontaneously as people understand what the load really is, and they collaborate to get the job done while playing their own part. The shadow, *look after your own turf,* reveals itself as in-company competition and narrow self-interest.

5 *Share the wins and losses* is the fifth and final practice, and reminds us that in big teams everyone wins and loses together, whereas in the shadow, *play I win, you lose,* people take credit for wins, while blaming losses on others.

As you reflect on the five practices in your organisation, notice how when one shadow is allowed to prevail, it begins to infect the others, and when one positive practice strengthens, it pulls the others towards it. For example, when people stop sharing the air it won't take long before they start to blame others and just look after their own turf. On the other hand, when people do share the air they develop a much better understanding of how they can support each other and that leads to shared wins.

As with most things in organisations, it is the quality of the leadership at all levels that is the key to creating teamwork across boundaries or energy-sapping silos.

Therefore, the following section explores how you can kick-start a think one team culture in your organisation by revealing the leadership requirements and some of the key strategies to engage others in the journey.

united leadership

What do putting a person on the moon, reaching the summit of Everest and winning an Olympic gold medal all have in common?

The answer, or at least one answer, is that they are each graphic examples of what are called 'superordinate goals'.

A superordinate goal is a goal that cannot be achieved individually but can be achieved collectively. In other words, an individual working alone cannot summit Everest, but this can be achieved by a group or team of people who work together towards that common goal.

Superordinate goals have been shown to reduce conflict and inspire cooperation in many settings around the world. For example, multi-ethnic communities in Sri Lanka have worked together towards the superordinate goal of building wells to provide drinking water, the Soccer For Life program in Honduras brings resources together to give children the chance to escape the perils of drugs and in El Salvador the superordinate goal to immunise children was endorsed by both sides in the combat and led to a ceasefire.

In the workplace, a superordinate goal can be government agencies working together to halve the crime rate in a city or a corporation combining all of its resources to take a new product to market faster and more efficiently than its competitors.

In the push for neatness in strategic and business planning the power of superordinate goals is too often forgotten or even dismissed in the quest for individual accountability. The goals tend to be department-focused, which puts the power in the individual kingdoms and their leaders, and therefore disempowers cross-functional teams and discourages partnerships across boundaries.

Superordinate goals inspire people, give meaning and ultimately create success for the whole organisation or system.

Remember the proposition at the beginning of the book, 'Imagine the possibilities when everyone in your organisation thinks and acts as one big team'. Imagine superior service, imagine fewer cost overruns on new technology upgrades, imagine more targeted sales campaigns, imagine better talent management, imagine faster commercialisation of new products, imagine anything and chances are you are thinking of a superordinate goal.

Creating a think one team culture is in itself a superordinate goal because it cannot be achieved by an individual but can be achieved by a united group of leaders.

Furthermore, when you have united leadership at all levels of the business you will find more superordinate goals.

As the O'Donnell's story illustrates, think one team is sparked by leadership—specifically, united leadership. Not surprisingly, then, a first crucial step in any think one team™ program is to understand and develop united leadership among the leaders of the organisation.

what united leaders do

United leadership is, firstly, the senior leaders setting the visible example of the five practices in their own actions as a team and then, secondly, bringing them to life through their leadership by:

- communicating a sense of purpose and direction (share the big picture)
- creating a feedback environment so people learn and grow (share the reality)
- engaging or involving people to tap the ideas and energy of everyone (share the air)
- collaborating and supporting, while playing their individual parts (share the load)
- seeking success together (share the wins and losses).

United leaders put the health of the whole organisation (or the combined entity if it is a joint venture) ahead of their own politics or agendas.

Some examples of these behaviours are explained in the table overleaf and contrasted with silo leadership.

united leaders	silo leaders
• Hold themselves and their colleagues to standards of behaviour—'team rules'	• Break the team rules for their own benefit
• Choose superordinate goals	• Choose narrow goals
• Talk about colleagues' strengths and see value in diversity	• Talk about colleagues' weaknesses and criticise their differences
• Talk openly about their intentions	• Hide their intentions
• Tackle the tough conversations	• Avoid tough conversations or play the personality, not the issue
• Make decisions and move on	• Debate endlessly for their own position
• Share and protect the united leadership philosophy	• Hold to their own leadership philosophy
• Use the language of 'we'	• Use the language of 'them and us'

creating united leadership

A great place to begin to think one team is developing united leadership behaviours among the executive team and their direct reports (or in larger businesses a divisional leadership team and their reports).

These senior leaders are in an ideal position to open the doors and windows of the silos. Starting with them is like preparing the paddock for sewing the crop. It creates a fertile environment for the think one team practices to grow.

An alternative is to begin by bringing two or more teams together from across boundaries to tackle a business problem or opportunity. This style of 'work-out' has the advantage of creating immediate evidence that think one team delivers tangible results and can be useful as a pilot program.

Whichever approach you take the 'make or break' will still be the leadership sponsorship and support.

understanding the five practices

practice 1: share the big picture

Many people talk about 'the big picture', but what does it really mean?

To envision what 'share the big picture' means think about the energy, focus and teamwork that happens when organisations or communities are in crisis. Suddenly people share the goals and values, act as one team, understand how to contribute and put their personal agendas aside.

Straightaway we can see that share the big picture is more than just an end goal or vision, although those are important.

A team that shares the big picture:

- makes sure that everyone knows what winning means and why it is important

- oozes fundamental values (respect, care, fairness, integrity) in its behaviour
- knows why each person's contribution is important
- thinks about the impact on others of what it does
- is energised by fulfilling its potential.

This is in contrast to 'pursue other agendas', where people:

- allow winning to mean different things to different people
- create the environment for individual and conflicting agendas to thrive
- fail to help people understand how they can contribute to a higher purpose
- rarely think about their impact on others
- are distracted from the whole team fulfilling its potential.

ideas to share the big picture

Not surprisingly, the most important activity is creating and communicating what the big picture actually is! This means creating a believable and emotionally compelling story that suits the audience(s).

create the story

Get your leaders together and have them draw diagrams or pictures that illustrate the big picture for the organisation. Forget the mission or vision statements at this stage because they too often lose their meaning in pointless 'wordsmithing'. The big picture is about the where (vision), why (the case) and how (values) of winning. Yes, 'winning', and it applies equally to the private sector, to government and to communities. It also applies to alliances. Winning can mean beating someone else but more often it's about achieving a standard or meeting a challenge.

Four questions that can be really helpful in defining the big picture are:

1 What is our superordinate goal or purpose?

2 Why is it important for everyone?

3 How do we intend to achieve that goal?

4 What are we not going to do?

The second question should include the 'harsh realities' that present the case for change, while the fourth question is important because it forces people to choose collectively how they will allocate their resources.

Be prepared to devote time to go beyond the usual 'mission, vision, values' presentation to create a story that is believable and emotionally compelling so that you get real engagement, not just nods of understanding.

define the behaviours

In some organisations the cynicism about 'values' has reached epidemic proportions, while in others the values are treated with the respect of commandments. If you are in the latter organisation, then that's great; however, for others the key is to begin a dialogue with everyone in the organisation about what behaviours are essential to being successful.

The advantage of focusing on behaviours is that they are specific, and people can easily see them in themselves and others.

Having an agreed code of values or behaviours is a key to working together across boundaries. It not only gives a common language, but most importantly there is a shared set of standards and guidelines for handling the ambiguous and difficult issues.

more 'miniaturising'

If a picture tells a thousand words, why do organisations continue to deliver their strategic plans in huge documents that are launched with fanfare and then land in someone's filing cabinet, never to see the light of day again?

Use the power of miniatures (that is, pictures, diagrams, metaphors, short narratives) to tell your stories and, more importantly, to engage people emotionally.

If you want to pursue this in more detail, the think one team™ tools from the website and in our programs will give you lots of ideas and assistance.

share the big picture questions

The following questions are excellent prompts to check whether you and your team are sharing the big picture:

- Does everyone know what success means?
- Are we thinking and acting end to end?
- Does everyone know why their role is important?
- Are we putting aside personal or business-unit agendas to do what is best for the whole organisation?

practice 2: share the reality

In the bestseller *Good to Great*, Jim Collins made the case that in great organisations people hold conversations that confront reality.[2] This ability to get the truth on the table

---

[2] J Collins, *Good to Great*, HarperCollins Publishers, New York, 2001.

in a constructive way is fundamental to maintaining the relationships that sustain across-the-organisation teamwork. It is also essential to doing things fast.

People who 'share the reality':

- speak the truth, respectfully and openly
- give clear, powerful feedback
- expect and embrace feedback
- keep people informed
- learn and adapt
- ask tough 'reality check' questions
- deal in facts
- tell people when they make a mistake.

In contrast, people who 'avoid and deny':

- put a spin on everything they produce
- make things more complicated than they should be
- sugar-coat their feedback to others
- fear receiving direct, honest feedback
- avoid the vigorous debate or play the personality not the issue
- deal in unsupported opinions
- cover their backsides.

ideas to share the reality

You can trust people who share the reality, but how can you team with people who avoid or deny the truth?

This ability to get the truth on the table is fundamental to tackling the important and often emotional conversations that are essential to think one team.

Following are some key ways to address reality.

tackle the tough conversations

It requires a mix of emotional intelligence and conversational savvy to tackle the tough conversations. Training all managers from team leaders to CEO in how to tackle the tough conversations is a great way to reduce the beating around the bush. Books such as *Fierce Conversations* also give a great insight into the skills that you need to really tackle the tough, emotional conversations.[3]

simplify the scoreboards

Most organisations have massive reporting processes that are more to do with risk avoidance than disciplined risk management. There are some steps you can take to reduce this unnecessary logjam:

- Take time to sort out the real measures that tell the truth about whether you are winning or losing.
- Put the measures onto a small 'dashboard' and make them visible to everyone, so they can see how the whole team is performing.

make feedback a way of life

There are many opportunities to make feedback a way of life in a business. Two that my team use extensively in think one team™ programs are:

---

[3] S Scott, *Fierce Conversations: achieving success at work and in life, one conversation at a time*, Viking, New York, 2002.

- *across the boundaries debriefs*. These are an opportunity for people to share feedback with each other. This can be an 'out-of-the-comfort-zone' experience initially, but with skilled facilitation it can be one of the most powerful ways to open up conversation and get people to speak the truth about things that have previously been taboo.
- *one team profiling*. We use a range of profiles to gather feedback. A favourite is the Team Management Profile (TMP), which was developed by the Australian-headquartered Team Management Systems <www.tms.com.au> and is used extensively in team development programs around the world. The TMP is a great tool for understanding your own and others' team styles and can be combined with colleague feedback to create a very constructive dialogue.

  From our own range of profiles the one team partnering scorecard is invaluable for measuring and monitoring the health of partnering between departments and functions. Details are available via <www.thinkoneteam.com>.

share the reality questions

The following questions are excellent prompts to check whether you and your team are sharing the reality:

- Are we getting the truth on the table or do people get surprises at meetings?
- Is everyone getting and giving feedback that matters?
- Are we tackling the tough conversations constructively?
- Do we have shared measures that give us an across-the-organisation scoreboard?

practice 3: share the air

The power of one team comes from tapping into everyone's ideas and energy to create an awesome team. That means giving people time to express those views and making sure that people know their responsibility is to be constructive.

The opposite of sharing the air is stifling communication and it has two sides to it.

First, it is dominating conversations and making communication one way, which stifles debate and leads to poor decisions with even poorer buy-in from the people who are expected to implement them.

Second, it is 'spectating' rather than participating constructively in discussions. The reasons for this are many, ranging from personal style to the habit of insecure managers and staff hoarding information.

Either of these two styles of communication starve the organisation of oxygen and cause people and teams to lose their edge.

People who 'share the air':

- actively listen to others
- accommodate others' views
- speak with clarity
- put alternative, challenging views
- treat people as equals
- create forums so ideas can be exchanged.

Whereas people who 'stifle communication':

- ooze cynicism in their comments
- speak over the top of others

- hoard their views
- preface comments with 'Yes, but'
- quickly dismiss alternative views
- use status to pursue their own agenda.

ideas to share the air

The essence of sharing the air is to remove the blocks to communication and to allow ideas, opinions and information to flow through the organisation. It is arguably the most powerful of the five practices in eliminating the damaging effects of silos because it builds partnering relationships across the silos.

Following are some key ways to share the air.

big team forums

Bring people together from across the organisation (at different levels) and engage them in discussing significant business issues. This process, described in the books *Future Search* and *Large Group Interventions*, can engage large groups of people in 'visioning' and problem-solving activities.[4]

responsibility to challenge

Team leaders can have a major impact on fostering openness by facilitating 'challenge meetings' in which people are coached in how to challenge constructively. We use the

---

[4] MR Weisbord & S Janoff, *Future Search: an action guide to finding common ground in organizations and communities*, 2nd ed, Berrett-Koehler, San Francisco, 2000.

BB Bunker & BT Alban, *Large Group Interventions: engaging the whole system for rapid change*, Jossey-Bass, San Francisco, 1997.

PROBED technique described in my book *High Performance Leadership* to give people a framework for inquiring into another person's viewpoint.[5]

calling cynicism

Few things are more damaging to sharing the air than people who take pride in showing their cynicism through their verbal and non-verbal behaviour. Most typical are the people who never say outright that they disagree, but their voice tone, facial expressions and body language all exude an energy-sapping cynicism. This behaviour must be 'called' by members of the team, by initially bringing it to the other person's attention. This might be done in an empathic way by saying, 'I'm not sure how things feel from your position, but from mine I'm receiving the message that you are cynical about what we are doing'.

share the air questions

The following questions are useful prompts to check whether you and your team are sharing the air:

- Do we have open forums where people can share the air?
- Is everyone involved and engaged?
- Are we open to alternative views and ideas?
- Are we leaving our egos at the door?
- Is active listening a feature of our meetings?

---

[5] G Winter, *High Performance Leadership: creating, leading and living in a high performance world*, John Wiley & Sons (Asia), Singapore, 2003.

practice 4: share the load

Sharing the load is where the work gets done and, arguably, it is the 'biggest' of the practices because it reminds us about the big picture and the many roles and tasks that are leading towards it.

Sharing the load means understanding what the load actually is and collaborating when needed to get it done efficiently and effectively.

The opposite of sharing the load is looking after your own turf. This is a common practice in business, partly because most organisations are actually designed (including the reward system) to encourage people to play to their own or their local team's agendas. This means that 'acts of teamwork' are needed on many levels to show that sharing the load is a better way to do business.

All too often teams mistake loyalty to their department or division for strong teamwork, while they unwittingly damage the overall organisation to achieve their own ends. This is easily justified, 'I am just doing my job'; however, it is poison for teamwork across boundaries.

When teams and individuals 'share the load' they:

- jointly plan and prioritise
- ask for help
- get the right people in the right jobs
- seek ways to collaborate and build understanding
- roll up their sleeves and help out
- simplify the organisation processes.

However, when teams and individuals 'look after their own turf' they:

- see others in the business as competitors
- spectate and criticise
- deny the need for help
- plan and prioritise by themselves
- duplicate processes and systems.

ideas to share the load

Following are some simple approaches and tools that can get you started sharing the load.

joint planning and prioritisation

The best way to reduce the complexity and angst that comes from having people looking after their own turf is to get them together early in the planning process and to prioritise jointly. Needless to say, this demands that they have the skills to share the air and share the reality.

It is amazing how people continue to protect their own patch by keeping others out until they have finished their plans, which then ends up creating mayhem for everyone else down the line. You see it between Manufacturing and Sales, between head office and regions, and between Information Technology and Business Units. It happens everywhere and it's dumb, so don't do it.

embrace simplicity

Businesses have a habit of growing much more complicated and complex than they need to. Get teams from across the business to challenge 'dumbplexity' and make things as simple as possible (particularly for your customers).

look left, look right (take off the blinkers)

When people understand what is happening up the line and down the line they are in a much better position to know how they are affecting other people's performance. Look left, look right means spending time in the areas upstream and downstream from your business area, so you (and they) can see how things have an impact on each other. When combined with some training or coaching in emotional intelligence a 'look left, look right' campaign can have a huge positive impact on freeing up the flow of work through an organisation.

share the load questions

The following questions are excellent prompts to check how you and your team can better share the load:

- Who can we involve in jointly planning and prioritising?
- What do we see when we look left, look right?
- Are we good customers and good service providers?
- Can we collaborate to get more leverage?

practice 5: share the wins and losses

When people think one team everyone shares the wins and the losses, which means that they know the score. This is important because in siloed organisations the score tends to be very local (related to just one department), rather than across-the-silo scores such as speed to market or end-to-end customer satisfaction.

The opposite of share the wins and losses is play I win, you lose. The people who have this mindset are of the view that as long as their area of the business is okay, then that's just fine by them. They can be found smugly noting that the Sales division is under target or a project team is struggling, while they have their department running to budget. Of course, as soon as things change, they will be the first to apportion blame to anyone from management to the courier company, just as long as it's not them.

Another version of this is not focusing on results at all because they convince themselves that it is the process they follow that is most important. From teachers to maintenance workers, and engineers to team leaders people rationalise processes but lose sight of the need to produce results.

When teams and individuals 'share the wins and losses' they:

- pay close attention to results (individual and collective)
- create the belief that everyone wins and loses together
- set goals or key performance indicators that encourage one team behaviours
- accept accountability
- celebrate the big and the small wins.

However, when teams and individuals 'play I win, you lose' they:

- ignore results that don't suit them
- look to blame others for defeats
- take credit for successes
- devalue the small wins
- make process more important than outcomes.

ideas to share the wins and losses

The most important step is to ensure that there are clear goals and scoreboards so that everyone understands and can see progress. This has been a key feature of many motor vehicle production lines for years as companies realised that people perform better when they are accountable for the whole result (in that case, the whole car) rather than just a small section.

Following are some ways to assist in creating these behaviours.

celebrate across the boundaries

Teams and departments are rarely good at celebrating their successes, which means that getting cross-functional teams together hardly ever happens. The good news is that by bringing people together to share the wins (such as winning a deal or launching a new product) you reinforce the importance of the value stream and have an immediate positive impact because it's so unexpected. Why not look left, look right and invite a few people to celebrate a recent achievement?

debrief relentlessly

The use of performance debriefing—with a focus on learning and adapting—is a great way to get people accustomed to dealing with reality and to focus on results. By regularly asking the following questions in a facilitated session you can create a more open, one team culture:

- What was supposed to happen?
- What did actually happen?

- What were the differences between expectations and reality?
- How can we learn and improve?

share the wins and losses questions

The following questions are helpful prompts to check how you and your team can better share the wins and losses:

- How do we know if we are winning?
- When did we last measure 'left and right'?
- What wins can we celebrate?
- Do our key performance indicators encourage one team behaviour?

does your business really 'think one team™'?

The questionnaire on the following page is a simple version of the think one team™ profile that is used in our programs. I have included the 'Think silos' section because it is a great way to reflect on how effectively people in your business really do practise teamwork across the boundaries.

More details on think one team™ surveys are available at <www.thinkoneteam.com>.

think silos assessment

Complete the following questionnaire to establish how often, in your day-to-day work, you see people displaying the silo behaviours that are described. Be honest, but don't dwell for too long on any one item.

Ratings

5–6 = Mostly/Always

3–4 = Occasionally/Sometimes

1–2 = Never/Rarely

Rating		It is typical in our business that people
① ② ③ ④ ⑤ ⑥	1	Put local agendas ahead of the big picture
① ② ③ ④ ⑤ ⑥	2	Lack understanding of people and functions across the business
① ② ③ ④ ⑤ ⑥	3	Rarely think about their impact on others across the business
① ② ③ ④ ⑤ ⑥	4	Avoid addressing the tough issues
① ② ③ ④ ⑤ ⑥	5	Sugar-coat feedback or don't give it at all
① ② ③ ④ ⑤ ⑥	6	Put a spin on everything instead of being real
① ② ③ ④ ⑤ ⑥	7	Speak over or dominate others
① ② ③ ④ ⑤ ⑥	8	Mistrust others
① ② ③ ④ ⑤ ⑥	9	Block or inhibit open communication
① ② ③ ④ ⑤ ⑥	10	Plan and prioritise in isolation
① ② ③ ④ ⑤ ⑥	11	Foster inconsistency in language and practices
① ② ③ ④ ⑤ ⑥	12	Keep resources to themselves
① ② ③ ④ ⑤ ⑥	13	Look to blame when things go wrong
① ② ③ ④ ⑤ ⑥	14	Fail to recognise the success of others
① ② ③ ④ ⑤ ⑥	15	Make process more important than outcomes

Scoring

Transfer your scores from the previous page, placing the score for each statement in the following table.

practice	statement	statement	statement	row score
pursue other agendas	1:	2:	3:	
avoid and deny	4:	5:	6:	
stifle communication	7:	8:	9:	
look after your own turf	10:	11:	12:	
play I win, you lose	13:	14:	15:	
total think silos score				

Interpretation

In each row you will have received a 'row score' of between 3 and 18, while you will have received a 'total think silos score' of between 15 and 90. The interpretation of these scores is provided in the following table.

total score	row score	interpretation
75–90	15–18	Across the boundaries teamwork is almost nonexistent and is likely to be seriously restricting your business performance. Your business needs to think one team urgently.
55–74	11–14	Poor across-the-boundaries teamwork is inhibiting your business. Consider using the five practices of think one team to address some fundamental realities and you should find many quick wins.
30–54	6–10	Your business has the potential to be a one team business. Why not leverage this potential?
15–29	3–5	You see your business as having a one team culture, which will enable you to operate with speed and agility. It is likely to be a competitive advantage for the business.

For details on the think one team™ profile, which provides a more comprehensive measure of leadership and team behaviour, visit <www.thinkoneteam.com>.

think one team™ program

Think one team™ is perhaps the most simple and powerful development program available to help organisations create the teamwork across boundaries that is essential to successfully executing their business strategy.

Each program is customised into action-based workshops and implementation projects led by accredited facilitators to ensure a defined business benefit.

what are the key programs?

think one team™ is currently offered in five core formats:

1 *think one team™ program*. This is a series of development workshops and projects for managers

and team leaders to embed one team practices in the business.

2 *think one team™ workout*. This is a workshop that tackles one or more specific business issues in a cross-functional team and extends into an implementation period.

3 *united leadership*. This is a program for senior leaders to ensure they are equipped to model and lead a one team business.

4 *think one team™ cascade*. This is an extension of the think one team™ program.

5 *think one team™ alliance workshop*. This is a customised program that brings together alliance partners to establish and/or strengthen the teamwork and collaboration.

In addition to these formats my team provides facilitation and coaching on issues that are important to creating and sustaining the benefits of a one team culture.

what resources support the program?

think one team™ is available only through our network of accredited facilitators and is backed by practical resources including this book, an extensive resource manual, simple and effective surveys and a range of desktop and meeting room merchandise:

- *think one team*. The story of The Big Jelly Bean Team is a quick, powerful and cost-effective way to introduce the think one team™ model and concepts to every employee in your organisation or to the members of an alliance.

- *think one team™ resource manual.* During the workshops a comprehensive resource manual is provided for every participant. This manual is designed to maximise the value from workshops and to act as a resource for the implementation phase. In a full program the manual features over 100 pages of information and activities from over fifteen modules.
- *think one team™ surveys.* A feature of think one team is the use of simple diagnostic surveys to measure how teams and individuals are living the five practices. These surveys range from the think one team™ profile, which is used to assess one team practices across the business, to the short one team partnering scorecard that provides vital information on across-the-boundaries teamwork. The latter is now incorporated into many corporate 'dashboards' as a key performance indicator.
- *think one team™ merchandise.* A range of products is available to support and reinforce the think one team message on the desktop and in meeting rooms. These products include posters, pads, feedback cards, 'how-to' guides and a host of simple tools to encourage across-the-boundaries teamwork. We even provide jelly beans as part of the workshops!

why think one team?

think one team™ programs deliver improvements in teamwork across boundaries, which lead to cost savings, faster new-product commercialisation, leaner business processes, reduced silos, better partnering and a host of other benefits.

The program has been conducted successfully in Australia, North and South America, Asia and Europe for whole organisations, and specific groups, including leadership and management teams, alliances and partnerships, and all manner of cross-functional teams.

I encourage you to imagine the possibilities for your business. For further information about think one team™ and the associated products, visit <www.thinkoneteam.com>.

summary

Few businesses can execute their strategies without:

- reducing 'silos' between business units
- uniting leadership teams
- driving key initiatives across the business units
- strengthening alliances and partnerships
- building consistent across-the-business team practices
- working together to tackle the 'tough' cross-functional issues.

Think one team™ is a refreshingly different way to tackle these issues. Its effectiveness lies not in complexity but rather in how the story of The Big Jelly Bean Team and the five simple practices engage everyone in an organisation to think and act in ways that create a better future.

I hope that this book and the think one team™ programs help and inspire everyone in your organisation to think and act as one big team.